From Stethoscope to Wisdom

Dr Andrew C S Koh

Published by Dr Andrew C S Koh, 2024.

Copyright

Scan the QR code above

Table of Contents

To my beloved wife, Wai Yin, whose love and unwavering
support have been the foundation of everything I do.

To my sons, who have brought joy and purpose into my life.

To my daughters-in-law, who have enriched our family with
their warmth and kindness.

To my grandsons and granddaughters, the light of my life,
who remind me daily of the beauty and wonder of the world.

And above all, to the glory of God, whose grace has guided me
through every step of my journey.

This book is for you all.

Healing the Body, Transforming the Soul.

Foreword

Dr. Andrew C.S. Koh's spiritual odyssey commenced in the modest town of Tanjong Malim, Malaysia, and persisted all the way through his retirement in Ipoh. Andrew grew up in a modest environment with non-Christian parents. He first encountered Christianity at a chapel service in elementary school, where he heard the parable of the prodigal son. This pivotal moment set him on an extraordinary journey of faith. As he navigated through life's challenges and triumphs, Andrew increasingly sought solace and purpose in his newfound beliefs. His passion for spirituality became a guiding force, influencing his interactions and decisions throughout his personal and professional life.

Andrew's education helped him overcome poverty and become a successful cardiologist. As a medical student, Andrew had a significant spiritual awakening that strengthened his commitment to Jesus Christ, especially during his time in Teluk Intan. This transformative experience deepened his understanding of compassion and healing, guiding him both in his personal life and professional practice. Andrew combined his faith with his medical career, aiming to meet the physical and spiritual needs of his patients.

He was fortunate to receive mentorship from two distinguished Bible teachers, which gave him a deep understanding of God's guidance throughout the Bible. I was honored to be his pastor at Holy Cross Lutheran Church, which made us close family friends. I saw Andrew's strong commitment to his faith and patients through our time at church and community service. His ability to blend spiritual wisdom with medical knowledge inspired not only me but also countless others around him.

Andrew is renowned for his unwavering commitment to his practice, beginning each procedure with a heartfelt prayer for his patients. He sees medicine as a way to share the Gospel with non-believers and help his Christian friends grow spiritually. His dedication is evident in his thorough study, teaching, and preaching of the Bible. He provides both physical and spiritual support whenever needed, not just at Holy Cross Lutheran Church, but also at other churches he visits. His influence extends far beyond the walls of the church, touching lives in ways that often leave a lasting impact. Every interaction allows him to show love and compassion, as he believes healing involves both body and soul.

In 1999, Andrew paused his medical career for three years to study at Laidlaw Bible College in Auckland, New Zealand, following what he believed was God's call. This book chronicles Andrew's extraordinary journey from childhood to retirement, highlighting the transformative power of faith in shaping lives when individuals choose to embrace and follow God's guidance. Through personal anecdotes and testimonials, readers will discover the challenges and triumphs he faced along the way. Ultimately, this narrative serves as a testament to the profound ways that faith can inspire change and foster community.

This book tells an uplifting tale of how God uses individuals, like Dr. Koh, as vessels within His kingdom. We extend our heartfelt wishes to him as he continues his ministry, whether through writing or preaching. His unwavering commitment serves as an inspiration to many, encouraging them to seek their own paths in faith. His contributions remind us of the significant impact one devoted person can have on a community and beyond. Every act of service, no matter how small, impacts the lives of others. It is this ripple effect of kindness and faith that can ultimately transform the world around us.

Pastor Paul Chong & Mrs. Ame Chong,
London, United Kingdom.
January 2024

Preface

Reflections on a Lifetime

This is a revised edition of my debut book, Memoirs of a Doctor, originally released in 2020. This book includes a lot of new material. With fresh chapters and poetry, along with thoughtfully rewritten passages, I have enriched the reading experience. Over the past few years, I have reflected on my journey, offering deeper insights into my life as a doctor. It is my sincere hope that these enhancements resonate with readers and encourage them on their individual journeys. The updates are designed to strengthen the connections to themes of resilience and compassion throughout my narrative. Each chapter highlights important events while celebrating the resilience of the human spirit in overcoming challenges.

This memoir shares my life journey, from my childhood memories to retirement. The book aims to inspire my family, friends, colleagues, and future generations, even as memories fade. I want to share the lessons and experiences that have shaped me, focusing on love, perseverance, and growth. Each chapter will serve as a reminder of the resilience of the human spirit and the importance of cherishing every moment.

For over five years, I've been thinking about writing my memoir. Due to my work commitments, I did not have the time or energy to write it. It was only after my retirement that I found motivation and the opportunity to continue. Now, with a renewed sense of freedom, I am excited to pour my heart into each page, weaving together the threads of my journey. This memoir will share my story and inspire others to pursue their own journeys with courage and hope.

My memoir writing journey was more enjoyable than I had anticipated. The first draft was completed in two months, but editing and proofreading took a longer time. Despite the setbacks, I learned to embrace the process, allowing the words to evolve and flourish as they were refined. Each edit helped me better express my experiences and connect more deeply with my story. Writing became a transformative experience, guiding me through reflection and self-discovery. With each change, I felt a new sense of purpose, as if I were discovering truths that had been hidden within me.

I dedicate this work to my late grandfather, father, mother, and uncle, who have all passed away. I'd also like to thank my wife, Cheah Wai Yin, my sons, Joseph, Joshua, and Joel, my daughters-in-law, Renee, Tina, and Angelina, and my grandchildren, Isaac, Benjamin, Daniel, Jonathan, Giselle, Katie, Annabelle, Isabelle, Kristabelle, for being a part of my life. Their unwavering support and love have been my guiding light, inspiring me to keep going even in the toughest times. This journey, woven with their memories and encouragement, will forever hold a special place in my heart.

I am grateful to God for His guidance and protection during my life's most dangerous moments. My daughter-in-law, Tina's unfailing encouragement and support have helped bring this project to life. Her belief in my vision pushed me to overcome obstacles and pursue my dreams with renewed determination. Tina's presence has been a constant reminder of the power of collaboration and love in achieving one's goals. Together, we have forged a path that not only fulfills my aspirations but also strengthens our bond as a family.

I extend my heartfelt gratitude to Dr. Timothy Sng, the late Canon Dr. S.K. Teoh, Lim Soo Ken, Dato' Dr. Gunasegaran, and Joanna Lee for their steadfast support and inspiration. I am very grateful for the guidance and mentorship from Dato KRR Naidu, the late Mr. Abel, the late Mrs. Jothi, and the late Mr. Nagappan during high school years. Their support and shared experiences have been instrumental in shaping my journey. Each connection has played a vital role in my growth, and I cherish the lessons learned from these remarkable individuals. These relationships highlight the importance of community and the positive effects of mentorship in life. Moving forward, I hope to honor their legacies by paying it forward and supporting others on their own journeys.

I sincerely thank everyone involved in creating and publishing this book. Your involvement and support have brought these pages to life, transforming them into a testament to our shared journey. As we move beyond these pages, I am excited to see how our paths will intertwine in the future. Together, we can continue to inspire each other and foster a supportive network that uplifts everyone involved. Let us take the lessons we've learned and apply them as we navigate our respective journeys ahead. With unwavering commitment, we can cultivate a community where growth and empowerment flourish for all.

Dr. Andrew C.S. Koh

Ipoh, Malaysia.

2024

Review

EXCERPT

Join Dr. Andrew C. S. Koh on an inspiring journey through his memoir, *From Stethoscope to Wisdom: A Doctor's Reflection*. This autobiographical account outlines his life from childhood to retirement. It focuses on key milestones and daily experiences that shaped his identity. Explore the 1950s, a time of close community bonds and personal interactions. Learn important lessons about resilience, connection, and wisdom from years of medical experience.

LEAVING A LEGACY

In *From Stethoscope to Wisdom: A Doctor's Reflection*, Dr. Andrew C. S. Koh shares his personal story of growing up and working in medicine until his retirement. This memoir is a legacy for his family and friends and inspires readers to think about their own lives. Koh's experiences highlight the crucial lessons of compassion and understanding in medicine.

Through his narrative, he encourages others to appreciate the small moments that shape our journeys and relationships. He shares stories and insights that show how practicing medicine is deeply connected to our humanity, not just clinical skills. Each chapter offers insights that connect with both the medical community and individuals on their own journeys.

By weaving personal anecdotes with professional reflections, Koh creates a tapestry of experiences that resonate universally. His memoir highlights that empathy and kindness are essential in healthcare and daily life.

He encourages readers to embrace vulnerability, highlighting how our shared experiences can create deeper connections. Through his journey, he illustrates that the essence of healing lies not just in treatments, but in understanding and compassion.

This approach redefines the relationship between caregiver and patient, emphasizing the importance of emotional support alongside medical skill. Readers are encouraged to think about their own stories and their role in the larger narrative of human connection.

REFLECTION OF THE 1950s

Koh takes us back to the 1950s, a simpler time when people connected in person. Community bonds have been instrumental in shaping individual identities. In this era, friendships were nurtured through face-to-face interactions rather than digital exchanges, fostering deeper connections. Koh highlights how these profound relationships laid the groundwork for resilience and support systems that continue to influence generations today.

Koh emphasizes how shared experiences were crucial for building resilience and a sense of belonging during this era. These connections, forged through everyday interactions, remind us of the value of genuine relationships in a fast-paced, digital world. As we navigate today's complexities, embracing these lessons from the past becomes even more vital. Koh encourages us to build meaningful connections in our lives to stay grounded in our shared humanity.

We see how strong and flexible people were back then. This highlights the need to keep personal relationships in a changing world. Koh's recollections serve as a reminder of the importance of resilience and adaptability in both personal and professional spheres. He shares insights from that era, encouraging readers to incorporate similar values into their lives to create lasting connections.

Through his experiences, he emphasizes that the foundation of any successful relationship is built on trust and understanding. By fostering these qualities, individuals can navigate the complexities of life with greater harmony and collaboration.

Moreover, Koh stresses the significance of open communication as a vital part in cultivating strong bonds. This approach not only strengthens existing relationships but also paves the way for new connections in an ever-evolving landscape.

LESSONS ALONG THE WAY

His journey into the field of medicine commenced in 1972. He reflects:

My journey into medicine began in July 1972, when I embarked upon an intense five-year undergraduate program and then one year of housemanship.

This includes being taught by *internationally renowned doctors like the late Prof. TJD.*

The memoir shares the key moments of his medical education. Koh highlights how each experience contributed to his growth, both as a physician and as a person. Through challenges and triumphs, he learned the importance of compassion and resilience in the face of adversity.

Each chapter unfolds with tales of triumph and challenges, revealing lessons learned along the way. From patient interactions to late-night study sessions, every moment left an indelible mark on his character. Ultimately, these experiences shaped not just his medical expertise but also his profound understanding of the human spirit.

Koh remembers that mentorship improved his clinical skills and gave him a deep sense of responsibility for his patients. He emphasizes that these foundational lessons continue to resonate throughout his career, shaping his approach to medicine and patient care.

One of the most emotional memories is about the tragic MH 653 air crash in 1977, which caused him to mourn the loss of a beloved mentor, stating:

He was a remarkable Obstetrics and Gynaecology professor, known for his kindness, excellent bedside manner, and generous spirit.

Koh's tribute highlights the deep impact that mentors can have on shaping his career and values. This poignant experience serves as a catalyst for his ongoing commitment to nurturing future generations in the medical field.

He is dedicated to teaching, mentorship, and sharing the wisdom he had gained. He learned from his experiences that challenges in the medical profession can lead to significant personal growth and understanding.

Through this journey, he has embraced the notion that every setback is an opportunity for resilience and innovation. His commitment to creating a supportive learning environment inspires many students to strive for excellence in their careers.

THE IMPORTANCE OF RELATIONSHIPS

Koh's reflections highlight the importance of personal relationships and community. He believes that strong connections with colleagues and patients create belonging and trust, which are crucial for effective healthcare. This foundation improves learning and promotes collaboration and empathy in the medical field.

He recalled an incident. He met one of his boy scout teachers in Labuan after a lapse of 2 decades.

The world is a small place came alive when I met someone in Labuan who recognized me but could not remember where we had met.

This sense of connections and shared experiences echoes throughout his narrative. He highlights that these connections enrich our lives and improve our capacity for compassionate care as healthcare professionals.

Koh's memoir highlights that the connections we make are essential to our personal growth. The memories we build are crucial for our professional growth.

EMBRACING RETIREMENT

After 48 years of dedicated service in medicine, Koh embraced retirement on his 68th birthday in 2020. He reflected on his career with gratitude for the meaningful relationships he built and their significant impact on his journey.

He looks forward to exploring new interests and strengthening community connections in this new chapter of his life. Koh sees retirement as a transition into a new phase with opportunities for learning and engagement. Koh aims to positively impact others while enjoying the freedom of retirement.

He concludes with a heartfelt sentiment:

Every day, I find an opportunity to reflect on the blessings I have received and to share His goodness with those around me.

This memoir captures a life of purpose and meaningful connections. Koh's journey serves as an inspiring reminder of the impact one person can have on the lives of many.

As he navigates this new chapter, Koh remains committed to fostering relationships and giving back to the community. His story is a testament to the enduring power of connection. It shows the fulfillment it brings in all stages of life.

Through his stories and reflections, he encourages others to cherish their relationships and actively engage in the world around them.

BLURBS

Archbishop Moon Hing Ng, Anglican Archbishop of Southeast Asia

Indeed, a truthful and insightful journey into the life of a doctor. This is a true, interesting, and colourful life story. It is about an ordinary person who becomes a cardiologist. This happens with the help and guidance of the One and True God, Jesus Christ. This book shows us that God is always there. He orchestrates and guides our journeys.

Rev. Ng Wah Lok, Ex-Principal of Tung Ling Seminary, Malaysia

Dr. Andrew C S Koh shares stories about his childhood, education, and a career in different towns. He also shares stories about marriage, family, the loss of friends, travels, love for the Bible, and paralysis.

Underlining the memoir is his faithfulness to God to live a productive land purposeful life.

CONCLUSION

From Stethoscope to Wisdom is a heartfelt look at a doctor's journey. It connects with anyone who appreciates the relationships that shape our lives.

Koh's use of personal stories alongside deeper insights makes this memoir engaging for anyone exploring their own life journey.

Through laughter and tears, he invites readers to ponder their paths and the impact of each meeting. This memoir reminds us that life is about the connections we make, not just the milestones we reach.

In a world often focused on achievements, Koh elegantly shifts our gaze to the profound moments that define our existence. Ultimately, his reflections serve as a powerful reminder of the beauty found in vulnerability and shared experiences.

By weaving together moments of joy and sorrow, he creates a tapestry of life that resonates on multiple levels. This exploration encourages readers to embrace their own vulnerabilities and cherish the relationships that shape their narratives.

In doing so, Koh invites us to think about our own stories and the connections that have influenced us. These shared experiences become the threads that bind us together, offering comfort and understanding in a chaotic world.

DISCOVER WISDOM

Dive into Koh's inspiring memoir and discover the wisdom garnered through a lifetime of experiences. Read *From Stethoscope to Wisdom: A Doctor's Reflection* today and find inspiration in the interconnected stories of triumph and resilience.

Through each page, Koh invites us to traverse the intricate landscape of human emotion. He reveals insights that can transform our perspective. Each story not only illuminates the path he has walked but also reflects the shared journey of us all.

As you turn the pages, you will find a mirror reflecting our own struggles and triumphs, encouraging empathy and understanding. Koh's words resonate deeply. They remind you that you are never alone in your experiences. The power of storytelling can unite all.

Testimonials

Archbishop Ng Moon Hing, Anglican Archbishop of Southeast Asia

Indeed, a truthful and insightful journey into the life of a doctor. This is an easy and interesting book and when someone picks it up to read, he will not put it down until the last page. A true, interesting, and colorful life story of an ordinary person who becomes a cardiologist with the help and guidance of the One and True God, Jesus Christ. This book shows us that though we may not believe or know God, He is always there to plan and script our lives. The author wished to share with his readers that when one does know this God, Jesus Christ, He will be even more ready to prepare and usher them towards the direction where they can find security, meaning, blessing, and joy. The panoramic view of a village boy to a city doctor, interspersed with beautiful poems, has shown how an honest, innocent young person faced and swam in the ocean of sophisticated and challenging turbulence. His faith in Jesus Christ has become an oasis for him in the world of struggles, unending expectations, and stressful pressures. A book of great relief and comfort for the soul.

Rev. Ng Wah Lok, Ex-Principal of Tung Ling Seminary, Malaysia

I found reading this book very inspiring as Dr. Andrew C S Koh shares stories about his childhood, education, a career in different towns, marriage, family, loss of friends, close encounter with paralysis, travels, and most of all his love for the Bible. The memoirs include some of his personal poems with the latest one about the Covid 19. Underlining the memoirs is his faithfulness to God, living out a productive and impactful life. At the end of the reading, you will find that God has been his faithful guide and shield all through his life.

Tina Chan

This book is an amazing story of one great cardiologist. Such an honour to be your daughter in law and a privilege to know you on a personal level, papa. A must read for everyone. A moving book as well as refreshingly candid that will be deeply inspirational to many.

Pastor Joshua Tan Poh Kong

A very inspiring and encouraging masterpiece presented enthusiastically and passionately. Clearly, the hand of God is with Dr. Andrew C S Koh and transforming him from a nobody into a giant for the Kingdom of God. Go forth, the best is yet to come. May you continue to be a blessing to many via your writings and other endeavours.

Dato K.R.A. Naidu

An excellent autobiography by Dr. Andrew C S Koh, my ex-student in Methodist English School Tanjong Malim way back in 1969. This book took me on a roller coaster ride through the turbulent time tunnel from 1952 to 2020, from Tanjong Malim across continents. It was undoubtedly an extraordinary journey of faith. It is an amazing chance to go back into the past to enjoy the memories from down memory lane. This experience is personally enriching and at times painful. A memorable, well-written, enjoyable, and lovely memoir to touch lives, Congratulations.

Dr. Robert Leong

Dr. Andrew C S Koh provided glimpses of his life through the years in a short, loveable, and easy-to-read book. I enjoyed his reminiscing about the kind of life he used to live in the cities and villages in Malaysia before the arrival of social media. His varied experiences as a government, private, and military physician were a novelty to read as well. I would have wanted him to elaborate more on some of the key events in his life, so perhaps there's room for a sequel or version 2.0

Dr Wong Che Hoe

A well-written Memoir by Dr. Andrew C S Koh, a friend for the past 30 years. It provides inspiration to all young aspirants who want to emulate Dr. Andrew C S Koh's footsteps to success both professionally and spiritually. Congratulations on the well-written and meticulous recapture of your life history in words. May God bless you abundantly.

Dr. Kevin

Such a sweet and colorful life you lead through with God being with you with or without your knowledge as He scripts your life. Amen and praise to Him!

Carol Chow

Dr. Andrew C S Koh has portrayed an excellent abstract of his life story defining significant times such as childhood and adolescence, and the times he was touched by the grace of God. It is an interesting book, full of the spices of life, touching, sad, and sweet reminiscences of his past that will stir the heart of any reader. It is extremely well-written with a few sweet little poems here and there. Passionate touches of God in his life gives great inspiration and encouragement to strive on.

Daniel Wong

Dr. Andrew C S Koh's book bears testimony to what the Word of God is saying to him even to this very day. There is no shadow of a doubt that he has heard the voice of the Lord Jesus Christ, our chief shepherd. I am truly encouraged, blessed, and touched by his testimonies.

Steven Hiok

Dr. Andrew C S Koh's memoir is a beautiful narration of his life story and journey of faith. It is written in simple English and the book is easy to read. You will be encouraged and inspired, as I was, by his stories and his life as a Christian.

J. S. Solomon

The story of your life can be summarised in one word AMAZING. I praise and thank God for you and all that you have done to spread the Gospel and the precious Word of God. My wife and I remembered you and your wife when you were in Taiping for a short while in the 1970s. May God continue to bless you and your ministry. Hallelujah! Praise the Lord.

Lim Seng Choon

The book consists of Dr. Andrew C S Koh's growing up years in Tanjong Malim, his pre-university in Telok Intan, and medical education in Kuala Lumpur. After that, he served at various government hospitals, and Malaysian Air force before continuing his specialisation in cardiology. He retired in January 2020. It is well written and easy to read. Congratulations.

Albert Cherk

Your book is very interesting, educational as well as inspirational. I admire the way you and your wife achieved so much in the medical and dental fields, raising such a wonderful family, apart from contributing to the Christian life and education in Malaysia, a rare feat indeed. You should be very proud of yourselves coming from a background not dissimilar to mine.

Dr Francis Ha

The life story of a dear friend and medical school classmate. From his humble beginning in a small village Tanjong Malim to his retirement as a cardiologist in Ipoh in 2020, his life, his career, his passion was and is moulded by God Almighty. God's hand was evident all the way through success and through struggles in his own life and the lives of a rather large, by present standards, family of 9 grandchildren from his 3 sons! A man of great belief, A man of great academia, A man full of love and care.

Chandran Krishnan Nair

Dr. Andrew C S Koh, my classmate from 1959 in Primary 1 until 1971 in senior high school, after which we took different paths but surprisingly met up again in Ipoh in 1987. The memoirs reiterate his unreserved faith in God that built up his perseverance to overcome obstacles and emit care and kindness to all around. The memoirs are also a recollection of memories and episodes that stretches from childhood stage until retirement. An interesting read that relates the troubles and tribulations encountered but which he overcame with sheer determination. Kudos to the great work.

J Sharmani

It was a very inspiring read about the author's humble beginnings, reaching great heights in his career, remembering God's providence and grace.

J R Wu-Whong

The author shared his interesting and colorful memoir with stories that show God's providence through life's struggles and challenges,

P. A. R.

The author shared his truthful and insightful journey in an easy, engaging, interesting manner, sharing stories about his childhood, education, a career in different towns.

Elizabeth O Carroll

This book introduced me to cultural life in countries I had no opportunity to explore. One scene that surprised me that of a woman who was swallowed by a crocodile while doing laundry in a river!

Valentina

An inspirational and heart-warming book about faithfulness to God reminding us to stay strong when the days are hard. The author reveals moments of his life in a motivational, educational, and engaging way.

S Jeyaratnam

A beautiful life story of the author and his childhood memories, overcoming many hardships to become a cardiac doctor.

Bob

Interesting snapshots of a doctor's life in cities and villages of Malaysia during the pre-social media era.

Rowan E. Creech

Took me back to the stories my grandmother told me of the days when she was growing up.

Jan Paessler

A concise memoir of the doctor's path from freethinker to Christianity, as well as his feeling of God's hand of provenance at key junctions of his life!

Texas

An interesting memoir of a Malaysian medical doctor. His childhood, his education, his family, his travels, and his faith and continued learning about God and the Bible.

T. Townsend

A perfect way to know the author, Dr, Andrew C S Koh.

Lulu

A detailed look at the author's long, interesting, purposeful, & miraculous life.

Fluffy Luggage

I found the author's life incredibly interesting, & he is a walking miracle!

A TALE OF TWO CITIES

A tale of two cities,
Tanjong Malim and
Auckland,
A tale of two countries,
Malaysia and New Zealand,
A tale of two tenses,
The past and the present,
A tales of two lives,
The flesh and the spirit,
A tale of two professions,
Cardiology and theology,
A tale of love and
providence,
A tale of persistence and
perseverance,
Walking and surrendering,
To the glory of God.

www.drandrewcskoh.com

Prologue

This book is an autobiographical narrative that chronicles my journey from birth to retirement. I wrote this memoir as a lasting legacy for my family, friends, and loved ones. In these pages, I share not only the significant milestones but also the everyday moments that shaped who I am. My hope is that my experiences will inspire and resonate with others who may find reflection in their own lives. I want to share lessons learned and wisdom gained through stories of triumphs and challenges. Each chapter serves as a reminder that our lives, intertwined through connections and shared experiences, are what truly define us.

This tale transports you to the 1950s, a time when society and daily life were still quite rudimentary. The waves of industrialization, computerization, and automation had yet to make their mark. In this simpler world, people relied heavily on face-to-face interactions and strong community ties that shaped their identities. As we explore this era further, we will uncover the intricate web of relationships and values that established the foundation for future generations. We will see how people demonstrate resilience and adaptability in their everyday lives amid change. Their stories will illuminate the importance of preserving human connections in the face of an evolving society.

Life moved at a more leisurely pace in those days. Correspondence was conducted via the postal service, which resulted in communication that took considerably more time than it does in today's fast-paced world. The book is structured into twelve chapters, each one capturing a pivotal moment in my life. Each chapter is enriched with photographs and poetry that resonate with its theme. These elements serve to deepen the reader's understanding and emotional connection to each experience. I want to weave a narrative and art together to showcase the beauty and complexity of life's journey.

The narrative unfolds across multiple chapters and culminates with my reflections on retirement in 2020. This book offers a wealth of valuable lessons. If it inspires readers to strengthen their faith in God, pursue excellence, overcome challenges, and succeed despite difficulties, it has achieved its goal. Each chapter is carefully crafted to resonate with the universal themes of hope and perseverance. Ultimately, my hope is that this work leaves an indelible mark on those who embark on this journey with me.

Through heartfelt stories and personal anecdotes, I aim to illustrate the power of resilience in the face of adversity. May these insights motivate others to pursue their own paths with courage and determination. As readers dive deeper into the narratives, they will uncover the transformative strength that lies within themselves. Embrace your unique journey; every small step contributes to your growth. Remember, each challenge you encounter is an opportunity for growth and self-discovery. Together, we will explore the myriad ways in which we can harness our inner strength to overcome life's obstacles.

MES CLASS OF 69

MES CLASS OF 69
42 years went by, in the
blink of an eye,
Grand reunion by the
riverside,
Brought back memories
of years gone by,
Memories of boy scouts
and girl guides,
Came scurrying by,
Emotions running high,
Karaokes, dances, wines,
and dines,
To keep the night alive,
Thank you for the
nostalgic night,
Of yesteryears gone by.

www.drandrewcskoh.co
m/poems

Chapter 1
Tanjong Malim

"It was the best of times, it was the worst of times"
– A Tale of Two Cities. Charles Dickens.

As a proud member of the baby boomer generation, I come from Tanjong Malim, a charming and unassuming town located in the Muallim district of Perak, Malaysia.. My story began in 1952, in this enchanting setting. Situated just 70 km north of Kuala Lumpur and 120 km south of Ipoh, Tanjong Malim is graced by the majestic Ulu Bernam River, which serves as a breathtaking natural demarcation. Growing up by the river, I treasured the simple pleasures of life, from playing along its banks to exploring the lush greenery that surrounded our community. The town's warmth and our close relationships shaped my early years and still influence me today. The memories of those carefree days, filled with laughter and adventure, remain etched in my heart. In Tanjong Malim, I learned important values like friendship, respect, and community that have guided me in life.

IF NOT FOR THE GRACE OF GOD

According to my parents, I came into this world in a shophouse that served as our residence. At that time, medical facilities and transportation were poor; there was no ambulance service, and we couldn't afford a car. When my mother went into labor, there simply was no time for us all to travel to a hospital before my birth took place. In the dim light of the shophouse, my mother endured the pain with strength I can only admire now, surrounded by family who offered support and love. My journey began in that humble place, highlighting my family's resilience and the blessings we received.

As fate would have it, I was born right at home, with my mother's best friend there to assist in the delivery. This serendipitous event cemented their bond even deeper, making them best friends from that day forward. I think God helped me get here safely. Without His help, I wouldn't be here today to share my life story with all of you. Growing up in such a close-knit environment, I developed a profound appreciation for the surrounding relationships. These early experiences shaped my understanding of love, support, and the importance of community in navigating life's unexpected twists. Looking back on those formative years, I remember the many moments that brought us together and created strong bonds that remain today. Each laughter-filled gathering and shared hardship deepened my belief in the power of unity.

PRAISING THE STARS

My grandfather named me "Chan Sing" in Cantonese, which means "praising the stars." He chose this name after seeing a bright sky full of stars one night. He wanted to honor the beauty of the stars by giving me this name. It symbolizes hope and guidance, reminding me to always strive for my dreams. Every time I look at the night sky, I feel a bond not just to my name but also to the love and dreams my grandfather gave me. This connection inspires me to reach for the stars, both literally and metaphorically. With each passing night, I am reminded of the legacy I carry and the dreams I aim to fulfill. This tale would eventually become known by my name.

My grandfather viewed me as one of the stars in the night sky. My name evokes the popular song "Starry, Starry Night". Thus began the tale of my arrival in this world and its beginning. This connection fuels my ambition and inspires me to shine brightly in all that I do. As I navigate through life, I carry his legacy with me, always looking towards the stars for inspiration. Each challenge I face serves as a stepping stone, guiding me through the darkness into the light. With every achievement, I hope to honor his memory and light the path for others who seek their own stars.

My name draws its inspiration from Abraham (Abram) in Genesis chapter 12. God promised Abraham an abundant posterity through which his legacy could continue onward. Like Abraham, I aspire to wholeheartedly embrace my calling, equipped with the strength and resilience necessary to achieve my purpose. In doing so, I aim to create a ripple effect, inspiring those around me to pursue their dreams and leave a lasting impact on the world.

"The Lord had said to Abram, "Go from your country, your people, and your father's household to the land I will show you. I will make you into a great nation, and I will bless you. I will make your name great, and you will be a blessing. I will bless those who bless you, and whoever curses you I will curse, and all peoples on earth will be blessed through you." Genesis 12:2-3

As the years passed without children of his own, Abraham became increasingly anxious. God revealed Himself to Abraham one day and made a divine promise. He said that Abraham's descendants would multiply greatly, like the stars in the night sky. This promise eventually led to the birth of Isaac. Isaac would become the child of the covenant, carrying forward the legacy that God had established with Abraham. This divine plan unfolded over generations, shaping the future of countless nations and peoples. Through Isaac, the promise would extend to his son Jacob, who would later be known as Israel. This lineage would become the foundation for a nation chosen to reflect God's purpose and glory in the world.

He took him outside and said, *"look up at the sky and count the stars if indeed you can count them." Then he said to him, "so shall your offspring be"* – Genesis 15:5.

UNIQUENESS OF TANJONG MALIM

Tanjong Malim is an extraordinary town situated at the intersection of two states, Perak and Selangor. Tanjong Malim is situated both in Perak and Selangor, with the Ulu Bernam River gracefully dividing the town into two. This river originally possessed extraordinary characteristics. The Perak side had clear water flowing downstream, while the Selangor side had muddy water flowing alongside. This natural division showcases Tanjong Malim's geographical uniqueness and its rich cultural diversity. The convergence of these contrasting waters symbolizes the blending of traditions and communities, creating a vibrant atmosphere that celebrates diversity.

Tanjong Malim is famous for its tasty dumplings, a culinary tradition passed down by a local family. This town is home to several important institutions. Sultan Idris Teacher's Training College, established in 1922, is now known as Sultan Idris Education University. Another notable institution is Proton City Township, where their car assembly plant was established in 1996. These institutions enhance local education and economy while fostering community pride. Tanjong Malim is a growing hub that attracts visitors and residents with its rich history and bright future. The blend of tradition and modernity is evident in its vibrant culture and annual events that celebrate its heritage. This dynamic environment not only nurtures academic excellence but also encourages entrepreneurial spirit among its inhabitants.

MY GRANDFATHER

My grandfather emigrated from China to Malaysia during World War II. Originally from Sei Wooi in the Guangdong district, my grandfather moved to Malaysia with his wife and their son, my father, seeking a better life away from the poverty they faced in China. He worked tirelessly to provide for his family, instilling in them the values of hard work and perseverance. His journey shows the resilience of those who sought new beginnings in foreign lands, shaping our family's story for generations.

Unfortunately, my father's younger brother was left behind in China to be cared for by relatives, so I never got to know him personally. Additionally, my grandmother passed away prior to my birth, so I have no knowledge of her or our connection. Even with their absence, my family's stories about them have filled the gap, illustrating their lives and sacrifices. I often find myself wondering how different our family dynamics might have been had they been part of our lives.

My grandfather made his living as a cobbler, running an individual enterprise to repair and refurbish shoes. However, alcoholism and opium addiction plagued his life, plunging him further into poverty. Yet despite these hardships, he remained kind-hearted, thus garnering my deepest affection. His resilience in the face of adversity taught me the importance of empathy and understanding in our family. I value listening to his stories about overcoming struggles; they inspire me to face my own challenges.

My grandfather would take me to the barber whenever my hair grew too long for his liking, instructing the barber to cut it short to suit his preferences, much to my dismay! With time, as he grew frail, his death deeply affected me; it was the first time someone so close to me had died, leaving a profound emptiness in my heart. In the days that followed, I found comfort in revisiting the memories we shared, with each moment echoing his voice and laughter. Although he's gone, his lessons will continue to guide me.

My mother originated from another town called Bidor. She came from an affluent family background; her father owned substantial plantations, land, and real estates. As one of six siblings (two boys and four girls), she held a special place as being her father's cherished daughter. She grew up in privilege and comfort but remained humble, which made her likable to many. This combination of wealth and humility shaped her values and profoundly impacted the family we evolved into.

My parents' union followed the customs of that time by being arranged through matchmaking. In the past, parents used to arrange marriages for their children as a common practice, which was different from how people choose life partners today based on love. Though it seems strange now, this was how relationships were created during that period of history. However, despite the absence of romantic love in the beginning, many were able to cultivate deep connections over time. This old-fashioned approach to marriage fostered a sense of stability and commitment that often blossomed into lasting partnerships.

NO 22, CHONG AH PENG STREET

My parents owned and operated a tinsmith business at No: 22, Chong Ah Peng Street, right in the town center. Surprisingly, the shophouse was still in its original condition until 2019 when it was dismantled and rebuilt. In 2018, I was given the unique honor of conducting a photoshoot of this same shophouse featuring all seven members who resided here back in 1958. It truly felt like divine intervention when all seven of us who resided here reunited for such a historic and exclusive photo session in Tanjong Malim! The atmosphere was filled with nostalgia as we reminisced about our childhood memories spent within those walls. Each captured moment served as a testament to our shared history and the unbreakable bonds we formed over the years.

We were all children in 1958, and I was just six years old when our first photographs were taken. For our 2018 photoshoot, each one of us faithfully recreated that same tableau frozen in time fifty years earlier. It was a beautiful reminder that although time had passed, the essence of our friendship remained as vibrant as ever. As we posed together, laughter echoed around us, weaving through the air like a warm embrace. At that moment, it felt as if no years had separated us, and we were once again those carefree kids, filled with dreams and boundless joy.

1958 (above), 2018 (below)

TOUGH BEGINNINGS

I have two brothers and one sister. I am the youngest. Sadly, my second brother passed away peacefully in Singapore in 2009. My eldest brother passed away in 2023. After this loss, only my elder sister remain. Despite the challenges we faced growing up, the bond we shared as siblings has always been a source of strength and comfort. We often remember our childhood adventures, which feel more valuable now that two of us are no longer here.

During their time in Tanjong Malim, my late parents had to endure significant financial strain. They lived in poverty due to slow trading for their tinsmith business, which happened during the economic downturn in Malaysia. They were burdened by debt and lived a hand-to-mouth existence, while practicing Taoist faith with idolatry and ancestor worship. Their resilience in the face of adversity taught us the importance of perseverance and gratitude. These lessons, rooted in their struggles, continue to shape our values and the way we approach life's challenges today.

Growing up in Tanjong Malim was difficult due to my family's extreme poverty. Malaysia faced a severe recession, causing commodity prices like tin and rubber to drop significantly. This made basic necessities, like food, difficult to afford and often required credit for purchase. Our family was among those living most precariously. We often relied on our community for support, sharing what little we had to get by. These experiences instilled in me a resilience and resourcefulness that I carry with me to this day.

My family resided in a rented shophouse. My father rented half the shop and one room upstairs. Additionally, a car repair shop rented the other half of the shop, which created noise and dirt. This made it difficult for me to study or find peace. I quickly adapted by creating a study space in the small upstairs room to focus despite the distractions below. This environment fostered my ability to concentrate and motivated me to strive for success amid challenges. Spending more time in my study area helped me discover my passion for learning and the joy of overcoming challenges. Each day became an opportunity to prove to myself that I could thrive, no matter the surrounding circumstances.

THE CURFEW

During the Malayan Communist Party insurgency, Tanjong Malim was subjected to a strict curfew. We had to stay inside during specific hours each day, which was a stricter lockdown than the COVID-19 restrictions. The curfew made people feel isolated but also encouraged reflection and resilience in the community. Amid the limitations, we found comfort in shared stories and experiences that brought us closer together. We learned to appreciate the little things, finding joy in the simplicity of our daily routines. Every evening, as the sun set, we gathered in small groups to share our thoughts, transforming the confines of our homes into a haven of connection and understanding.

One vivid memory I have from that period involves my late father cooking pigeons for our meals. Surprisingly, we had pigeons living in our home; they arrived spontaneously, and after we started feeding them, more began to flock in. It became a sort of ritual, where each meal felt like a celebration of our unexpected guests and the warmth they brought into our lives. Watching my father cook with care and passion nourished us and strengthened our family bonds, reminding us of the importance of love and togetherness during tough times.

My late parents also raised chickens, ducks, geese, and turkeys as part of our farm operation. Each Christmas, they would present the estate manager client with a turkey as a gift. They also grew vegetables for home consumption. They always took care of all their children's needs, even when they were facing financial difficulties. They never let us go hungry or without proper sustenance. Their dedication to our well-being instilled a strong sense of family values and resilience in us. We learned the importance of hard work and the satisfaction that comes from nurturing both the land and those we love. This foundation shaped our approach to life, prompting us to cherish every meal and appreciate the effort behind it. Now, as adults, we carry those lessons forward, striving to create a similar nurturing environment for our own families.

GOOD TIMES IN BIDOR

I spent most of my holidays in Bidor, where I had a great time with my cousins. They were the children of my mother's older brother, her older sister, and her younger sisters. We used to spend time together during school holidays. We had the most wonderful moments together, playing timeless childhood games like marbles, catapults, catching spiders, spinning tops, flying kites, and countless others that were all the rage back then. We often explored the nearby jungle, finding hidden trails and creating stories about secret treasures. Those carefree days filled with laughter and imagination remain some of my fondest memories. Tanjong Malim to Bidor is 62 kilometers apart, taking about 45 minutes by car or 1.5 hours by bus.

My late uncle, my mother's older brother, cherished me for my dedication to my studies. As a result, he often presented me with new watches; an impressive gesture given their high cost at that time. He was an outstanding saxophonist who played by ear instead of reading music. He performed at weddings, funerals, and private events, and also played at home. He was like Bidor's version of another popular international saxophonist. His passion for music inspired me to appreciate the art form in all its nuances. Listening to him brings back warm and nostalgic memories of our close bond. His melodies would linger in the air, evoking emotions that words could never capture. In those moments, time stood still and the world faded, leaving only the sound of his saxophone.

My uncle, a projectionist at a movie theater, frequently treats my cousins and me to watch movies for free. Chinese New Year celebration in Bidor included fireworks and red envelopes filled with money from all our relatives. My aunt and uncle prepared breakfast and dinner for us every day, making our stay enjoyable and memorable. The warmth of family gatherings and shared laughter created a sense of belonging that was irreplaceable. As we reminisced over cherished memories, we discovered how deeply intertwined our lives had become.

THE FLOOD

I clearly remember the devastating flood that hit Tanjong Malim in 1971. The entire town was inundated, reaching waist-high levels at our shop. It took days for floodwaters to recede, leaving behind damage to furniture and equipment as they did so. Consequently, cleaning up and returning to normalcy required immense efforts and hard work on our part. Yet, through the chaos and disarray, our community rallied together, united by a common purpose. The experience not only strengthened our bonds but also instilled a sense of resilience that would shape our future endeavors. As we navigated the recovery process, we discovered new ways to support one another and foster growth within our community. This determination motivated us to rebuild both our spaces and the sense of togetherness that defines us.

IMPETUS TO SUCCEED

My parents strongly believed in superstitions. They trusted traditional Chinese medicine, believed in the healing power of mediums, and regularly participated in Chinese temple worship. The exposure to different cultures made me really want to get a good education. It's my way out of poverty and my chance of having a better future for me and my siblings. I studied diligently, using every resource available to me, determined to break the cycle of hardship. With each small victory in my education, I felt a renewed sense of hope for a brighter tomorrow.

My upbringing fostered an early ambition of mine - becoming a doctor. Since I was young, I wanted to provide care based on science instead of superstition. The two general practitioners near my late father's shop inspired me. Their compassion and dedication ignited a passion within me to help others in similar situations. I imagined walking these hallways in a white coat, making a difference for those in need.

According to my parents, when I was only a baby I contracted measles. I almost died from high fevers and dehydration, but luckily my fever went down with divine intervention and I survived. Now, I can share my story with all of you. Through this experience, I've come to understand the fragility of life and the importance of access to medical care. I want to pursue a career in medicine to help others facing their struggles. Inspired by my own journey, I aim to be a source of hope and healing for patients and their families. My experiences have ignited a passion within me to advocate for healthcare accessibility for everyone, regardless of their circumstances.

SCHOOL DAYS

During my time at Methodist English Primary School from 1959-1964, I have hazy memories of my primary school years. However, one specific memory from my first day remains vivid. That morning, my parents secretly put onions and sugar cane in my school bag to try to boost my intelligence. They also believed this would make me sweet, as sugar cane is naturally sweet. When I entered the classroom, the unusual smells from my bag caught my classmates' attention.

I felt embarrassed when a classmate saw onions and sugar cane in my bag. He started laughing loudly, which made me feel humiliated and unsure of what to do. Yet eventually this classmate became my closest pal for most of my primary school years, sharing many adventures. We bonded over our shared love for silly pranks and exploring the nearby woods after school. Those moments became some of my fondest memories, reminding me how unexpected friendships can blossom in the most unlikely situations.

We often went to the library to read books and listened to pop music on the radio. We loved listening to the pop songs of the 1960s. He imitated the late King of Rock and Roll by combing his hair high.

He was known by the nickname Poppy Leong. We would spend hours laughing and sharing stories, feeling like we were living in our own little world. Those carefree days filled with music and friendship created a bond that would last a lifetime.

We played with spinning tops, catapults, and marbles. We captured fighting fish from the rivers and gathered spiders from the trees. We flew kites, rode bikes, played games, and participated in Boy Scout movement activities. Each adventure brought us closer together, weaving memories that would forever hold a special place in our hearts. As we grew older, those moments became the foundation of who we were, shaping our dreams and aspirations. Through laughter and shared experiences, we learned valuable lessons about friendship and resilience. Our carefree days of exploration sparked a curiosity that led us to seek new adventures everywhere.

One day, however, my best friend suddenly left school without any warning, depriving me of the chance to say goodbye or find closure. He said he would move to Seremban with his parents in the future but didn't provide a new address or notify me. This left me devastated. Days turned into weeks, and the absence of his laughter echoed in the hallways where we once shared secrets and dreams. I longed for the day we would reunite, cherishing our friendship as a precious jewel. As time passed, I often found myself reminiscing about our adventures, feeling a bittersweet mix of nostalgia and sorrow. I held on to the hope that one day, our paths would cross again, allowing us to rekindle the bond that meant so much to both of us.

After losing contact with him for 48 years, we miraculously reconnected in 2015 through Facebook, Google, WhatsApp, email, and other social media platforms. He decided to move and retire to Jakarta. I traveled to Jakarta twice just to meet him again. I was surprised at our second meeting because he had forgotten many things, like onions, sugar cane, hairstyle, and even his old nickname, Poppy Leong. A few memory lapses can't overshadow the nostalgia that our warm conversations revive, reminding me of our carefree days together. It was clear that while time had changed us, the bond we shared was still worth rekindling. As we reminisced about our shared adventures, I felt a deep sense of gratitude for the moments we had created. Even as his memory faded, the emotions of our friendship stayed strong, showing the lasting power of true connection.

At this point, it is with sadness that I must share that six years after our reunion my dear friend died from lymphoma. Though his passing is sad, I'm grateful that God allowed us to reconnect; it was a special opportunity. In his final days, we often spoke about our dreams and the laughter we once shared, filling our conversations with warmth and love. I hold onto those memories tightly, knowing they will forever be a part of the tapestry of my life. As I reflect on our time together, I find comfort in the lessons he taught me about resilience and friendship. His spirit continues to inspire me, urging me to cherish each moment and embrace the bonds we create with others.

ENCOUNTERING THE GOSPEL

During my primary school years, I had a free period every Friday morning. I chose to attend chapel services that were held at our school church during this time. On a Friday morning, the late Mrs. Jothi masterfully expounded the story of the Prodigal son from Luke 15:11-32. Her storytelling captivated me, highlighting the gravity of choices and the depth of forgiveness. It was a moment that forever changed my understanding of grace and redemption in my life. That day, the message of unconditional love and acceptance sparked a desire in me to explore my faith more deeply.

A father had two sons; one older, righteous one, and another younger one who tended toward waywardness. The younger son received his inheritance, left town, and wasted it all on extravagant things. Eventually, he ended up bankrupt and taking care of pigs. Finally, he regained his senses and chose to go back home. I was so surprised when his father warmly welcomed him and even threw a big

38

celebration in his honor! In this parable, the father represents God, and the prodigal son represents those who have strayed but are still loved by Him. This story serves as a powerful reminder of forgiveness and redemption. It highlights that no matter how far one may wander, the path back to God's grace is always open. In this way, every individual has the opportunity to seek forgiveness and start anew. It inspires me to offer the same grace and compassion to those around me.

The story of the prodigal son deeply affected me and made me reflect on my relationship with God, despite my independent mindset. On this day, the message of the Gospel was sown into my heart.

ROLE MODEL BROTHER

Being in the Boy Scouts taught me important leadership skills. Chan Wing, who was two years older than me, was not only an outstanding King Scout but also served as a Head Prefect. He was both my role model and mentor. Teachers and scoutmasters held him in high regard as a student. He exemplified dedication and responsibility, qualities that inspired everyone around him. Watching Chan Wing navigate challenges with grace motivated me to strive for excellence in my own endeavors. I often sought his advice, eager to learn from his experiences and insights. His encouragement fueled my ambition and helped me find my own path toward leadership.

Chan Wing's achievements in the Boy Scouts inspired me to join and succeed in the movement. As an inseparable pair, I gained many life lessons from him. Due to his influence, scoutmasters and teachers also extended guidance, training, and assistance directly to me. This collective support nurtured my growth and instilled confidence in my abilities. With each challenge I faced, I felt more capable and empowered to lead others. This support has been crucial in helping me become a leader who can inspire and uplift others.

THE SCOUT'S JOURNEY

I started in the Scout movement as a private and moved up the ranks by passing tests and earning badges. Each experience shaped my character, pushing me further along my journey of personal and professional development. I started by passing the Tenderfoot badge and quickly advanced to more challenging ones as I progressed. With each badge earned, I not only acquired new skills but also learned valuable life lessons about perseverance and teamwork. These achievements became milestones that marked my growth and commitment to the values embodied in scouting. As I continued to climb the ranks, I took on leadership roles that taught me the importance of communication and responsibility. These experiences molded me into a more confident individual, ready to face new challenges and inspire others along the way.

Scouts needed to show skills in knot-tying, identifying trees, birds, and flowers, and also in swimming, hiking, trekking, and jungle survival. After much hard work, I earned the prestigious King Scout badge with the help of my scoutmaster's guidance. This accomplishment felt like the culmination of my dedication and effort, symbolizing a significant chapter in my scouting journey. Wearing that badge with pride made me realize that the friendships and experiences gained along the way were just as valuable as the awards themselves. I realized that every challenge faced and skill learned shaped my character and strengthened my connections with other scouts. As I moved forward in my journey, I was eager to take on new adventures and share the lessons learned with others.

CAMPFIRES & CAMPING

My favorite part of scouting was always campfires and camping adventures. Our campsite was chosen along the banks of the Sungei Bill River. The soothing sound of the water flowing nearby created a perfect backdrop for our evening stories and songs. Sitting around the fire, surrounded by friends, I felt a sense of belonging that deepened my appreciation for the outdoors and the connections we formed in those moments. Each flickering flame drew us closer together, illuminating faces filled with laughter and anticipation for the stories yet to be told. These nights became a cherished tradition, where memories were woven into the fabric of our friendship under the starlit sky.

Once we reached the campsite, our first order of business was to set up tents. In preparation for possible rain, we dug a trench around each tent; typically, each tent could comfortably house four people. Interestingly enough, many large rocks emerged from underneath the river's waters as landmarks to the campsite. Their unique shapes and sizes sparked our imagination, leading us to create stories about each one. As darkness fell, the flickering flames cast playful shadows on the rocks, adding to the enchantment of the night. We gathered around the campfire, sharing laughter and tales under the starry sky. The cool breeze wrapped around us like a comforting blanket as we roasted potatoes and savored the warmth of camaraderie.

Dinnertime at our campsite was always an incredible experience. The senior scouts took charge of preparation, expertly boiling rice and making curry chicken with potatoes. They would prepare dishes like fried noodles and vermicelli rice noodles under the supervision of our scoutmasters. I have a vivid memory of the delicious chicken curry rice dish that we had during my boy scouts' adventure. We sat on large rocks, surrounded by beautiful scenery like flowing rivers and waterfalls. The serene ambiance transformed the mealtime experience into something truly memorable. As we savored each bite, laughter and stories filled the air, bonding us as friends and scouts. Those moments instilled in me a love for outdoor cooking that I carry with me to this day.

After dinner, we enjoyed a fun campfire with singing, guitar playing, games, sharing stories, and making memories. A highlight from that time included *"It Only Takes a Spark"* and *"Kumbaya'*. The melodies fostered a spirit of camaraderie, resonating through the night like a warm embrace.

At night, we took turns guarding the campsite to keep it safe from animals like wild boars or other creatures. Under the starlit sky, we felt a connection to nature and each other that would always remain in our hearts. We didn't often see snakes, but we had to deal with leeches and mosquitoes a lot. On lucky nights, we could spot owls peering out from within the darkness!

Staying awake through our shifts required consuming strong black coffee throughout the night. We kept a campfire burning to keep us warm and repel mosquitoes and other insects. We also used Wellington boots to keep leeches away while we patrolled with torches.

At night, the jungle was filled with an incredible orchestra of sounds, creating an extraordinary and captivating ambiance. Above us was the beautiful night sky filled with the moon and stars.

SECONDARY SCHOOL

Since I wasn't particularly good at sports, I focused on my studies instead. To make up for it, I did well in school by consistently being one of the top students in my class. I was often chosen as a school prefect, a class monitor, or involved in different academic roles. These responsibilities helped me develop leadership skills and a sense of accountability. I enjoyed being a role model for my peers and took pride in contributing positively to the school environment.

As I think back, I remember winning book prizes and cash awards almost every year, making my parents very proud. Those achievements motivated me to continue pushing myself academically and personally. Every accolade boosted my confidence in the importance of hard work and dedication for a bright future. I realized that these experiences shaped not only my academic journey but also my character. Each challenge I faced became a stepping stone, leading me to discover my true potential and aspirations.

As I went through secondary school, I often engaged in activities that may not have been wise. I went on hitchhiking trips twice with a fellow Boy Scout. We wanted to earn our King Scout badges by traveling from Penang to Malacca. I didn't have enough money with me, and I knew my parents wouldn't approve. I didn't inform them beforehand or tell them about these trips. In addition, I used to swim in the Simpang Empat River with my friends without notifying my parents beforehand. The thrill of adventure overshadowed any lingering guilt I felt for keeping secrets from them. Each adventure felt both freeing and frightening, making me feel more alive than ever.

On a particular swim session, I experienced severe leg cramps that almost led to my drowning. Thank God someone came quickly to pull me from the water just in time, averting disaster. Reflecting on this event now, I realize that it was yet another instance of divine intervention saving my life. Since that moment, I've become more determined to embrace life's unpredictability and cherish every fleeting moment. Each day feels like a reminder of how precious my existence truly is.

PETS & HOBBIES

I also had pets. They say that dogs are man's best friend. I found this saying to be true through my own observation. I had a beloved mongrel named Bobby. When he came home as a puppy, he quickly stole my heart with his friendly nature and his constant playfulness. However, as he got older, his needs became too much for me to handle. Eventually, I had to give him up. It was one of the hardest decisions I ever made, but I knew it was what was best for him. Letting go was painful, but I hoped he would find a loving home that could meet all his needs.

Since I couldn't take care of Bobby, I decided to give him away to a farmer to look after his farm. I blindfolded him and took him to a nearby farm in his new owner's truck. But to my surprise, two weeks later, Bobby came running back to me. He was dirty, hungry, thirsty, and tired. I cried tears of joy when he came back after I had sent him away. From that day on, I took care of him until he died. Bobby became my constant companion, always by my side, and his loyalty reminded me of the bond we shared. Those moments together filled my heart with warmth, and I knew I would cherish his memory forever.

Bobby wasn't my only pet. I also owned two monkeys, a male, and a female, quite an exotic group! I also liked reading books by famous writers like William Shakespeare, Robert Louis Stevenson, Mark Twain, Charles Dickens, and Enid Blyton, among others. Each author transported me to different worlds, enriching my imagination and fueling my love for storytelling. With Bobby and my monkeys by my side, I often found myself inspired to weave my own tales full of adventure and friendship.

One day, after reading Swiss Family Robinson, I built my own treehouse at the back of the house. Every evening after dinner, I would climb up to my treehouse to read books. It became my own safe place where I could escape from the world. As I settled into my temporary refuge, the swaying branches created a calming melody that enhanced my reading experience. In that magical place, my imagination was limitless, and I felt like the captain of my own ship, ready to explore new territories.

OTHER RECOLLECTIONS

My memories of past incidents remained vivid. A Malay woman was tragically eaten alive by a crocodile while washing clothes on the bank of the Ulu Bernam River. This shocking event surprised the whole town. Fear spread through the community as the river, once a life-giving source, now served as a reminder of nature's power. The tale of the woman served as both a tragedy and a warning, echoing in the minds of those who lived near the water's edge.

There was yet another tragic incident that affected a train passenger. His head was accidentally severed when he leaned out of the window while passing through a narrow bridge. After this incident, someone pretended to be a ghost to scare nearby residents until the police caught and charged him. The pranks only heightened the town's anxiety, as the specter of death seemed to linger over them. Whispers of the supernatural made people avoid the river and its surroundings, fearing what might be hidden beneath.

In 1969, during my fifth year of secondary school, a devastating fire engulfed Behrang Station near Tanjong Malim and reduced an entire row of shops to ash. I remembered going with one of my classmates to his house after school and finding it completely destroyed. Thankfully, his family was able to evacuate before their home was completely engulfed. The sight of the charred remains haunted me for weeks, a stark reminder of how quickly life can change. Standing among the ruins, I felt the town was trapped in a cycle of misfortune, causing unease in our hearts.

As part of my school days, I would often cycle from Tanjong Malim to visit friends in the neighbouring towns, Kalumpang, Behrang Ulu, and Behrang Station. We would travel together, enjoying conversations along the way while pedaling swiftly when passing near graveyards in the late evening. We pedaled quickly out of fear of supernatural beings lurking nearby! The thrill of racing past those eerie shadows only added to the excitement of our adventures. Those carefree days felt like a distant memory now, overshadowed by the lingering specter of loss that enveloped the town.

An Indian scoutmaster in his forties vanished under mysterious circumstances. His family has no clear idea what happened to him. There were speculations that he might have been kidnapped and killed by communist insurgents in the jungle. The community was on edge, whispering about the dangers lurking just beyond their familiar surroundings. As the sun set each evening, the once vibrant trails felt eerie, echoing the untold stories of the missing.

On a more upbeat note, I was actively engaged with a band known as Asteroid, where I served as a guitarist. Our band had five members, including myself as the rhythm guitarist. We also had a lead guitarist, a bass guitarist, a drummer, and a singer. We performed at different events like school talent shows, weddings, and private functions. Each gig was an opportunity to connect with the audience, sharing our passion for music and creating unforgettable moments. The energy from the crowd always fueled our performances, reminding us why we loved to play together.

Recently, our band experienced a partial reunion when three of us, myself included, came back together as a 3-piece band at our MES Class of '69 annual reunions in 2018 and 2019. Unfortunately, one guitarist from this line up passed away due to liver cancer in 2020. His loss affected us all deeply, both personally and musically, as he was essential to our sound and spirit. The memories of our time together lingered in every note we played, a bittersweet reminder of the bond we shared.

SOJOURN IN KUALA LUMPUR

After I finished my Form 5 exams in 1969, there was a nervous wait until our results were announced. A group of friends and I decided to work at a bakery in Kuala Lumpur to gain experience and pass the time. However, the experience turned out to be challenging and tiring. Long hours and the heat from the ovens tested our endurance, but we learned valuable lessons about responsibility and teamwork. Despite the challenges, we formed strong bonds that would last a lifetime, making the experience memorable.

At times, our working conditions were exploitative, with meager wages and long hours. Work usually begins at 8 a.m. and ends around 10 p.m., with breaks for meals and snacks throughout the day. Tasting the bread I made was an unforgettable experience after all the hard work I put into it! After our shifts, we would go to the worker quarters in the bakery complex to rest before starting work again. The teamwork among the workers helped us manage the exhaustion as we shared stories and laughter during breaks. Despite the challenges, our dedication to our craft kept our spirits high, fueling our passion for baking.

At my bakery job, I developed relationships with several co-workers. There was a situation where a handsome man was interested in a beautiful neighbor girl. They both liked each other, but there were differences in their backgrounds. He came from a poor background and had little education, while she belonged to the middle class. These differences kept them apart. Despite their attraction, they hesitated to act on their feelings, fearing judgment from their families and friends. However, the connection they felt was undeniable, and they often found themselves stealing glances at each other across the bakery.

After the bakery stint, I found out about their troubled relationship and how it eventually ended. The boy subsequently left Kuala Lumpur, separated from his partner, and unfortunately became addicted to drugs. When I heard about this, I was deeply saddened. It was a stark reminder of how quickly life could spiral out of control. I wished I could have reached out to him before it was too late, hoping to light a spark of hope in his dark times.

THE STORY CONTINUES

That was my first job earning a pay check as a bakery worker in bustling Kuala Lumpur. I remember the warm scent of freshly baked bread in the shop while I learned to knead dough and decorate pastries. Every day was a chance to improve my skills, but I couldn't shake the worry about my friend's well-being.

In 1969, I embarked on a journey from Tanjong Malim to Teluk Intan, located 86 kilometers away in Perak, to pursue my Form 6 education. I lost contact with most of my classmates from Methodist English School (MES) after leaving Tanjong Malim, except for those who also went to study in Teluk Intan. Reuniting with them brought a wave of nostalgia, as we reminisced about our carefree days together. The sense of friendship motivated me to succeed in my studies and make new memories with my old friends.

In 2015, we created a WhatsApp messenger chat group for the MES Class of '69. We used platforms like Facebook, Google, WhatsApp, email, and social media to reconnect and establish this group. We had our first big reunion in 2016 at the Shah Alam Club.

After that, we had annual reunions in 2017, 2018, and 2019. Each gathering revived happy memories and strengthened our connections, letting us reminisce about school days and share our life stories. The laughter and stories shared at these reunions brought us joy and strengthened our long-lasting friendships.

Within our larger group, a smaller subgroup embarked on various overseas journeys, visiting destinations such as Perth, Jakarta, Medan, Lake Toba, and Vietnam. We used to gather for special occasions like Christmas, Chinese New Year, Hari Raya, Deepavali, and birthdays. However, because of COVID-19 pandemic, our activities have decreased since 2020. We hope to resume them when the situation gets better. As we look ahead, the anticipation of reconnecting and creating new memories fills us with hope. With each passing day, we remain hopeful that we will soon gather again to celebrate our enduring connections and the joy of being together. In the meantime, we find solace in virtual gatherings, sharing stories and laughter through screens. These moments remind us that distance cannot diminish the love and bond we share as a family.

Band

HMSS CLASS OF 70

HMSS Class of 70,
40 years after leaving the city,
Teluk Intan by the sea,
Participants came back for a reunion,
Involving many nations,
Memories came flooding back,
Unable to hold the emotions back,
Give me more songs and wines,
Karaoke, dance and dines,
Into the dead of the night,
Thank you for the nostalgic magic,
Of yesterday once again!

www.drandrewcskoh.com/poems

Chapter 2
Teluk Intan

"It was the age of wisdom, it was the age of foolishness, it was the epoch of belief, it was the epoch of incredulity, it was the season of light, it was the season of darkness, it was the spring of hope, it was the winter of despair."
– *A Tale of Two Cities, Charles Dickens.*

I lived in Teluk Intan for two years, from 1970 to 1971, while attending Horley Methodist Secondary School (HMSS). During my first year, I was in lower Form 6, and in my second year, I was in upper Form 6. This two-year education journey provided opportunities to explore numerous fields. I participated in various extracurricular activities that broadened my horizons and developed my leadership skills. The friends I made during this time remain an essential part of my life, shaping my experiences even today.

TELUK INTAN

Teluk Intan is a small town in the Lower Perak District of Perak. It has a population of 128,179 people as of 2016. The town was originally known as Teluk Mak Intan, or Mak Bay. It has undergone several name changes. Teluk Anson was the next name, followed by Teluk Intan in 1982. The name Teluk Intan reflects the town's historical significance and maritime heritage.

Teluk Intan, a town primarily known for its agricultural activities, is home to a number of colonial-style buildings. Teluk Intan's renowned iconic leaning building is a 25.5 meter tall clock tower that looks like a pagoda. It leans to the left and stands at a height of 25 meters. This tower is known as the Malaysian equivalent of the famous Leaning Tower of Pisa, located in Italy. Visitors to Teluk Intan are often captivated by its unique architecture and historical charm. The town also offers a vibrant local market where residents and tourists can enjoy traditional cuisine and crafts.

During my first year in Teluk Intan, I lived with my aunt's family, with my uncle and cousins. The family provided me with food and lodging, making sure I was taken care of. Living with them allowed me to immerse myself in the local culture and traditions. I quickly learned to appreciate the warmth of family ties and the rich flavors of home-cooked meals. Every evening, we would gather around the dining table, sharing stories and laughter while enjoying the diverse dishes prepared by my aunt. This experience deepened my connection to the community and made me feel like an integral part of their lives.

The following year I moved into a homestay closer to the school with another family. This new environment was more conducive to studying, since many of my classmates lived in the area. Being on my own gives me a sense of freedom, autonomy, and independence. I quickly adapted to the routines and customs of my new family, learning to appreciate their unique perspectives and traditions. As I settled in, I found myself forging lasting friendships that would shape my high school experience. I joined various clubs and activities, which made it easier to connect with others who shared similar interests. Finally, the sense of community and belonging I felt began to fill the void with homesickness I'd initially experienced.

MY TIME AT HMSS

Horley Methodist Secondary School (HMSS), Teluk Intan was a rich heritage dating back to 1899 when established by Reverend W.E. Horley. Horley also founded Anglo-Chinese School Ipoh in 1895 to provide a complete pre-University education experience. The school has a long-standing tradition of academic excellence and community involvement, which has endeared it to generations of students. As I explored the history of HMSS, I felt proud to be part of its legacy, knowing I was walking the same halls as many who had come before me.

The teachers at HMSS Teluk Intan were friendly, knowledgeable, and always willing to help students. Approximately ten of my former classmates from MES Tanjong Malim joined me in pursuing our education at HMSS Teluk Intan. Some girls from the Convent School Teluk Intan and some boys from the neighboring towns, Tapah, Bidor, and Sungkai also became part of our HMSS family. Together, we formed a diverse community that enriched our educational experience and fostered lifelong friendships. The collaborative atmosphere inspired us to excel academically while simultaneously engaging in various extracurricular activities.

My memories of Teluk Intan are somewhat foggy as I can no longer recall specific details from that time. At HMSS, I had the privilege of being a School Prefect and President of the 6th Form Society. As part of this role, we published monthly newsletters and annual magazines. These publications allowed us to highlight our achievements and share important information with the school community. It was a rewarding experience that taught me valuable skills in leadership and communication.

In Teluk Intan, I had a close friend who was a student from Bidor. He joined HMSS in 1971 and became one of the top students. We shared a room in our homestay and experienced many adventures together. His sense of humor, tall stature, fair features, charming manner and intellect made for unforgettable friendship. We spent countless nights talking about our dreams and ambitions, forging a bond that would last a lifetime. Our shared experiences not only deepened our friendship but also shaped the individuals we would become.

We participated in various activities, including publishing newsletters, playing games, cycling, listening to music, and enjoying outdoor pursuits. I have outgrown the activities I used to enjoy in primary school, like playing with spinning tops, marbles, catapults, fighting fish, flying kites, and catching spiders! Those childhood memories are dear to me, reminding me of joyful and uncomplicated times. As I moved forward into adulthood, I embraced new passions that reflected my evolving interests and aspirations.

REAL INTERACTION SANS SOCIAL MEDIA

Back then, we didn't have things like the internet, mobile phones, tablets, e-mail, WhatsApp messenger, or Google. Instead, we relied on personal, face-to-face communication, which allowed for more meaningful interactions between people. Adulthood has brought a plethora of responsibilities, making life more complex and less simple compared to the past. Our guiding philosophy was "*eat, drink and be merry for tomorrow we die.*" There wasn't the need to schedule appointments to meet; meetings happened spontaneously and adhoc. Laughter and shared experiences were the cornerstones of our gatherings, creating bonds that felt unbreakable. In simpler times, unexpected visits from friends or spontaneous gatherings created our fondest memories.

I continued playing the guitar solo but did not join any bands. Surprisingly, I didn't join the Boy Scouts at HMSS and chose to practice Tae Kwon-Do in the evenings instead. During that time, I tried different games and sports, but I didn't achieve much in athletics. However, I was a great student and always ranked among the top students in school. My dedication to academics often took precedence over extracurricular activities, but I found joy in learning and exploring new subjects. This passion for knowledge shaped my character and prepared me for the challenges that lay ahead.

TRAGEDY IN 1970

I vividly recall a tragic event from 1970 when one of my classmates took his own life by hanging. He recently shared that he felt like a failure and struggled with being unpopular and inadequate in his studies. He felt unloved and disrespected because he hadn't received any important roles in school society. His loss impacted our small school community, highlighting the often-overlooked issue of mental health struggles. This incident sparked a discussion about the importance of kindness and support and helped me understand the unseen struggles that many people deal with.

He envied my popularity and desired to swap places. There was something profoundly saddening in his demeanor, with an accompanying sense of despondence. He was seen carrying ropes around our neighborhood in the days before the tragedy. When it happened, it deeply affected all of us at school. We didn't expect this to happen, even though we knew there were warning signs. In hindsight, I realize I should have been more supportive in urging him to get professional help sooner. However, it is now clear that this might have changed what happened, but unfortunately, it didn't. The weight of missed opportunities looms heavy over my memories. I am left grappling with a mix of guilt and regret, wondering how I could have made a difference.

GOSPEL SEED SOWN

At HMSS Teluk Intan, there was one classmate who embraced Christianity and became my role model. He shared God's love through Christian fellowships that I attended. There, I enjoyed meeting new people while enjoying fellowship, shared stories, and refreshments. It provided transformative insights that have the potential to change lives! These gatherings showed me how faith can transform my life and the lives of those around me. Each meeting was a reminder of hope and inspiration, encouraging me to explore my own beliefs more deeply.

Despite my doubts and reservations, the Gospel touched my heart and grew, even though I initially resisted it. Eventually, it became stronger. Still, I remain eternally thankful to my friend who introduced me to Christianity. His unwavering support helped me navigate my spiritual journey, making me realize the importance of community in fostering growth. Together, we celebrated milestones and navigated challenges, solidifying a bond that transcended mere friendship.

At HMSS, one of my classmates developed schizophrenia in our second year. Over time, he became increasingly religious, proclaiming himself to be Jesus Christ sent by God to save humanity. Unfortunately, his psychosis worsened to such an extent that it made continuing studies impossible. Looking back, I should have advised him to seek professional medical assistance earlier. Schizophrenia is a treatable and manageable disease after all. Eventually he left school, and I lost contact with him. I often wonder how he is doing and whether he ever received the help he needed. The memories of our time together still linger, reminding me of the fine line between brilliance and madness. It's a haunting reminder that sometimes the most brilliant minds can slip into shadows unnoticed. I hope he found his way back to the light, surrounded by support and understanding.

JELLYFISH ENCOUNTER

A pleasant Chinese lady science teacher in my last year of high school organized incredible nature study trips. She took us on a trip to Pulau Sembilan, also known as Nine Island Resort. We spent three days and two nights there, doing nature study activities on the beach and by the sea. It was a beautiful and peaceful place, perfect for doing assignments and bonding with fellow students. One day, while exploring the shores, we stumbled upon a swarm of jellyfish gracefully drifting in the clear waters. Their translucent bodies shimmered in the sunlight, captivating us and reminding us of the wonders of marine life surrounding us.

There, I was stung by a jellyfish and my leg swelled up almost instantly. Luckily, the swelling went away quickly and I didn't have any serious consequences. Despite the scare, it became a memorable part of our adventure, bringing us closer as we shared stories and laughter. That day, we learned to appreciate not only the beauty of nature but also the unexpected thrills it can bring. As the sun set, coloring the sky orange and pink, we sat by a beach fire, reflecting on our day. The sound of waves crashing on the shore provided a calming backdrop, concluding a memorable experience perfectly.

MEETING MY FUTURE WIFE

Looking to supplement my homestay expenses, I decided to offer private tuition. One day, unexpectedly, a friendly Chinese girl from Convent School approached me and asked if I would tutor a Form 4 student at her home. To my amazement and surprise, this marked the start of two years of tutoring a student. Little did I know then that this young lady would later become my wife. As I started tutoring her, our connection deepened, and the time we spent together became the highlight of my days. Each session was filled with laughter and learning, laying the foundation of a beautiful relationship.

HAND OF PROVIDENCE

My time in Teluk Intan became exciting when I participated in a key exam for entering university. I was accepted into University Malaya Kuala Lumpur, one of Malaysia's top medical schools, due to my excellent exam performance. The late Professor Emeritus Tan Sri T. J. Danaraj was the Dean of the Medical School. His dedication to molding future doctors inspired countless students, including myself, to strive for excellence. Under his guidance, I felt a renewed sense of purpose in my journey towards becoming a physician.

Perak State Scholarship was an immense help, covering my tuition fees and living expenses from 1972 to 1977. This grant was much-appreciated, since my parents had limited means to support university education on their own. Even more remarkably, one of the interviewers for this scholarship interview happened to be my father's friend. This connection gave me confidence during the interview and highlighted the value of community and support in education. I'm thankful for the opportunity and motivated to honor my family's sacrifices and the faith others have in me.

During the interview, he was kind and made me feel at ease with straightforward questions, which made me feel hopeful about getting the scholarship. I received the HSCE examination results and the scholarship award notification. Then, I had to wait for six months before starting university studies in July 1972. Those months were filled with excitement and anticipation to embrace this new chapter in my life.

At that point, I stayed with my sister and brother-in-law in Ipoh. They had completely embraced Christianity, marking a significant change for both of them. While I was home alone, I began reading the Bible, focusing specifically on the Gospels of Matthew, Mark, Luke, and John. I wanted to understand its message and gain perspective on its teachings. The words I read made a strong impression on me and deepened my spirit. As I delved further into the scriptures, I found myself reflecting on my own beliefs and values. Each passage seemed to resonate with my experiences, guiding me toward a more introspective journey of faith.

After leaving Teluk Intan, I unfortunately lost touch with my former classmates from HMSS. However, we were able to reconnect in 2016 through social media platforms like Facebook, Google, WhatsApp messenger, and email. WhatsApp and Facebook remain the channels through which we maintain contact with one another. However, many classmates remain untraceable even until now. Despite the digital tools at our disposal, some memories seem to fade away like whispers in the wind. The bonds we shared remain in our hearts, reminding us of our unforgettable moments together. It's a bittersweet reminder of how time and circumstance can alter connections. Yet, those cherished memories continue to inspire us and shape who we are today. We carry their essence with us, woven into the fabric of our experiences. As we move forward, we honor those connections by creating new memories that reflect the growth we've achieved.

HMSS Teluk Intan

Leaning Tower of Teluk Intan

MU CLASS OF 72

MU Class of 72,
39 years after leaving
medical school,
Doctors from many
nations,
Came back to the same
station.
Memories came flooding
back,
Unable to hold our
emotions back.
Singing, dancing,
drinking, and dining,
Into the dead of the
night,
Thank you for the
nostalgic night,
Of yesteryears gone by.

www.drandrewcskoh.co
m/poems

Chapter 3

University of Malaya

"A dream, all a dream, that ends in nothing, and leaves the sleeper where he lay down, but I wish you to know that you inspired it."
– A Tale of Two Cities, Charles Dickens.

I lived in Kuala Lumpur for six years while studying medicine at the University of Malaya. After my fifth year, a housemanship opportunity presented itself at what is now known as University Malaya Medical Centre (UMMC). This experience was invaluable as it helped me apply my theory in a real setting, greatly improving my practical skills. Working alongside experienced professionals, I encountered various cases that further fueled my passion for healthcare and patient care.

A DREAM REALISED

I achieved my lifelong goal at the University of Malaya's Faculty of Medicine. The faculty was founded in 1962 and is highly respected by medical professionals around the world. I joined Malaysia's top medical school as its ninth batch of students. It is well-known globally and highly respected within medical communities around the world. The curriculum was rigorous and challenging, pushing me to grow both academically and personally. Each lecture and clinical experience enhanced my understanding of medicine and strengthened my commitment to improving patients' lives.

My journey into medicine began in July 1972, when I embarked upon an intense five-year undergraduate program and then one year of housemanship. I always wanted to become a doctor. It would give me a stable career, a better quality of life, and a reliable income. I wanted to help those in need by providing assistance and offering support to people going through difficult times, relieving their suffering and pain, and giving them hope and comfort. Thanks to divine providence, this dream became reality. God always looked out for my interests and well-being! Every step of my journey was filled with challenges and sacrifices, but my passion for healing kept me motivated. Now, as I stand in my medical practice, I feel a profound sense of purpose and fulfillment.

1st RESIDENTIAL COLLEGE

In my first year, I resided at the 1st College; a residential college situated conveniently close to the Faculty of Medicine. From there, it was only a quick walk or motorbike ride away until classes began after a week-long orientation process. The friendships I formed with my peers made starting medical school a supportive and motivating experience. We shared late-night study sessions, explored the campus together, and forged friendships that would last a lifetime. The college community fostered collaboration, inspiring us to succeed both academically and personally. I had no idea that these early connections would become invaluable sources of support during the challenges we would face in our medical journey.

On my first day at medical school, the respected Emeritus Professor TJD, the Dean of Medicine, spoke to our class of 72-77 in the impressive clinical auditorium. His words remain imprinted on my mind: *"Medicine is an ongoing journey and never just five years in medical school."* His assertion that what we had learned would quickly become obsolete upon graduation was proven correct in hindsight. The challenges and complexities of medicine require lifelong learning and adaptation, which I embraced wholeheartedly. Every day in medical school served as a stepping stone, rich with invaluable experiences that shaped my understanding and passion for the field.

1st College was far from impressive when it came to food, serving similar uninspiring meals every day. Luckily, however, there was a Chinese food shop on campus where I could occasionally enjoy some Chinese fried noodles! These little moments of culinary delight became a refreshing break amidst the rigors of studying. They satisfied my cravings and reminded me that even busy days can have small joys.

Each bite of the savory noodles brought me comfort and nostalgia, helping to alleviate the stress of exams and clinical rotations. In those brief moments, I realized that self-care is crucial on the challenging path to becoming a doctor.

PROFESSOR T J DANARAJ

The late Professor T.J. Danaraj highlighted the significance of ongoing learning for doctors as medical knowledge rapidly evolves. He likened doctors to pilots, emphasizing the necessity of regular practice. I recall him commenting, *"if you want plenty of money right now, please find another course."* Medicine needs calling and passion to succeed. His words deeply resonated with me, emphasizing that true fulfillment in this profession comes from genuine dedication instead of financial goals. As I continue my journey, I strive to embody that passion and commitment to lifelong learning.

Prof. TJD was a highly respected clinician and academic who set high standards while remaining friendly and approachable. His ability to balance professionalism with warmth created an inspiring environment for all of us. I hope to carry his lessons with me as I navigate the challenges of my own medical career. The values he instilled in us will serve as a guiding light during difficult times. With every patient I encounter, I aim to honor his legacy by approaching each situation with empathy and unwavering dedication.

MENTORED BY THE BEST

The medical school curriculum was divided into two modules. The preclinical module, lasting two years, covered fundamental sciences such as anatomy, physiology, biochemistry, parasitology, pathology, clinical pharmacology, public health, and medical statistics. Although it may seem overwhelming, this knowledge is vital for understanding and practicing medicine safely and effectively.

The clinical module gave us hands-on experience in patient care, allowing us to use our basic knowledge in a real-world setting. This transition not only bolstered our confidence but also solidified our commitment to becoming compassionate healthcare professionals. Throughout this journey, we were mentored by the best in the field, learning invaluable lessons from experienced physicians and professors. Their guidance shaped our understanding of complex medical concepts and instilled in us the importance of empathy and patient-centered care.

Our class had 128 medical students who were some of Malaysia's top students. We were lucky to be taught by internationally renowned doctors like the late Prof. TJD. Their extensive experience and passion for teaching inspired us to excel in our clinical practice. This hands-on experience solidified our understanding and application of medical principles in real-world scenarios. During our rotations, we met a variety of patients, each one challenging us and testing our skills. These interactions not only deepened our clinical knowledge but also reinforced our commitment to advocating for patients' needs and well-being.

The late Prof. TJD emphasized the significance of regarding every patient as a unique individual, acknowledging their name and humanity, instead of just seeing them as a case number. He emphasized that success in medicine relies on knowledge, honesty, ethics, empathy, compassion, kindness, and good bedside manners. These lessons have become guiding principles that we carry with us into our future practices. We aim to honor his legacy by upholding these values in all our patient care as we begin our careers.

Students often find case conferences with the late Prof. TJD to be intimidating. Each time, one student presented a case to the class, anticipating questions and potential criticism from classmates and professor. Everyone, including those who didn't have cases, were nervous because the late Prof. TJD would randomly call on students and expect them to ask insightful and intelligent questions. This pressure fostered a vibrant learning environment, where critical thinking thrived amidst the tension. In retrospect, we realized that these challenging moments were essential in shaping our confidence and competence as future healthcare professionals.

Prof. TJD often diagnosed his patients quickly by observing them during bedside rounds, without needing to ask about their medical history or perform physical exams. He stressed the importance of being observant and using all five senses to make accurate diagnoses. This involves conducting thorough history-taking and physical examinations. By honing these skills, we became better equipped to identify subtle signs that might otherwise go unnoticed. This holistic approach to patient care enhanced our education and prepared us to be more effective and empathetic healthcare practitioners.

Prof. TJD distinguished himself during a ward round when he diagnosed Chronic Rheumatic Heart Disease (CRHD). The diagnosis included checking the pulse, inspecting the jugular venous pressure waveform, looking for leg swelling, finding the position of the apex beat, and feeling for vibrations on the chest. Auscultation of the heart using a stethoscope was only an additional confirmation step. His clinical acumen transcended both cardiology and neurology. He seamlessly integrated knowledge from various disciplines, demonstrating how interconnected bodily systems can influence patient outcomes. This experience enhanced our understanding of complex conditions and motivated us to take a broader approach in future work.

Medicine was taught as both an art and science. Mastering the art of medicine needs qualities like empathy, compassion, kindness, ethics, and a connection with patients, beyond just scientific training. The art of medicine transcends mere science altogether. It invites us to actively listen and engage with patients on a deeper level, recognizing their unique narratives and experiences. This holistic perspective is essential for fostering trust and collaboration in the healing process. Furthermore, integrating human experience into clinical practice enriches the doctor-patient relationship, leading to better health outcomes. A physician who understands the emotional and psychological dimensions of illness can provide more personalized care and support.

A MEDICAL STUDENT'S LIFE

My life as a medical student was dramatic, fast-paced, and exciting. There were many things to learn, many skills to acquire, and relationships to nurture. The preclinical years were long and challenging, involving lectures, biochemistry lab work, and group anatomy dissections with cadavers. Seeing a cadaver for the first time was not as frightening as what television dramas portrayed. The dead bodies had been preserved with embalming fluids, so it smelled strong in the anatomy laboratory! Despite the initial discomfort, I found myself captivated by the human body's complexities and the intricate systems that sustain life. Each dissection enhanced my appreciation for the medical field and fueled my growing passion for it.

My anatomy professor stressed the importance of our shared dissection experience and respect for the cadavers. This experience brought our group closer together and helped us develop a deep respect for each other. Through laughter and shared moments of reflection, we bonded over our fascination with the marvels of human anatomy. Each lesson about life and mortality was a powerful reminder of our future role in caring for human health. Exploring the body's complex systems made me appreciate the blend of science and compassion that characterizes medicine. This journey strengthened my commitment to becoming a physician and inspired me to positively impact my future patients' lives.

ENCOUNTERING JESUS

My class had a Christian fellowship group with 12 Christian classmates who had converted prior to enrolling in medical school. Initially an atheist, I was warmly embraced by this Christian community. They invited me to their weekly lunches and other events, sharing Christian literature and offering personal prayers. As I spent time with them, I found myself drawn to their faith and the sense of belonging they provided. I started to explore my spiritual beliefs and a deeper connection with God through meaningful conversations and shared experiences.

While spring-cleaning, I found a Christian book. The letters were adorned with heartfelt messages and signatures from my dear Christian friends. It made me emotional as I remembered how these connections influenced my faith. Through their guidance, I became acquainted with Christianity. I felt an overwhelming sense of gratitude for the community that nurtured my spiritual journey. This discovery inspired me to reach out to them once again, to reconnect and share my evolving beliefs.

In 1976, during my fourth year of study, I experienced a personal crisis. During a difficult time, someone from Varsity Christian Fellowship (VCF) came to my room and talked to me about his belief in Christ. As a result, I chose to become a Christian. This pivotal moment transformed my life, igniting a passion for faith that had previously lain dormant. It marked the beginning of a profound journey filled with exploration, learning, and connection with others who shared similar values. Through VCF, I found a supportive community that nourished my spiritual growth. We discussed, volunteered for different causes, and learned how to live our faith in daily life.

My relationship with one particular classmate known for his long beard was special to me. He was an academic from Sarawak and his nickname was "janggut" which means beard in Malay. We shared similar wavelengths and enjoyed each other's company. Unfortunately, in later years he began to see a girl more often, which caused our time together to lessen. I understood that relationships evolve and priorities change, but I still missed our conversations and the bond we had developed. Even though we are far apart, I wish him happiness, as those memories will always be special to me.

RECONNECTION

The student whom I tutored in Teluk Intan entered the University of Malaya as a dentistry undergraduate in 1974. We were able to quickly come together again since we both lived in 1st Residential College. We were both awarded the prestigious Perak State Scholarship! Our shared backgrounds and experiences allowed us to easily rekindle our friendship. While at university, we often reflected on our experiences in Teluk Intan, identifying shared goals and challenges. As we navigated our rigorous coursework, we supported each other through late-night study sessions and shared vital resources. These events not only strengthened our bond but also enriched our university experience, turning challenges into moments of growth.

CONCLUDING THE CLINICAL YEARS

For my final three clinical years, I relocated to the Clinical Student Hostel (CSH). At CSH, students had a close bond, but there were times when some students could be mischievous. I recall an incident where a student chose to pour red paint on a college warden's car as an act of revenge against him. This stunt caused a lot of trouble and led to disciplinary meetings we all wanted to avoid. It reminded us of the thin line between friendship and chaos, showing the importance of responsibility as we grow up. The experience taught us that while camaraderie is essential, it must be balanced with maturity and respect for others. Ultimately, those moments became a memorable part of our journey, shaping us not only as students but also as individuals prepared to face the real world.

Even during exams, some classmates engaged in late-night card games and gambling yet still managed to excel academically. Many students wore dark-tinted glasses in the back rows of lecture halls to sleep during class. This peculiar mix of rebellion and responsibility highlighted the diverse approaches to education and life among my peers. The chaotic yet lively atmosphere fueled my growth, showing that learning often happens beyond traditional limits. During those vibrant years, I learned the importance of balancing a carefree attitude with diligence, allowing me to find my unique paths amid the chaos. Reflecting on these experiences, I realized they would always influence my identity and the relationships I built.

As some classmates drove newer BMWs, most of our professors could only afford older Volvos or Peugeots. The difference in financial status was clearly evident. It served as a reminder that success is not solely defined by material wealth, but also by knowledge and character. This realization made me appreciate my peers' diverse backgrounds and the valuable lessons they contributed to my experiences together. I found strength in the connections that transcended wealth, forming bonds based on shared struggle and triumph. These relationships broadened my view, showing that true success comes from connecting and supporting each other through various situations.

BY THE GRACE OF GOD

Although I wasn't an outstanding student, medical school presented considerable challenges - reading, memorization, comprehension, and conceptualization were required. By God's mercy, however, all examinations were successfully passed, and I graduated with an MBBS (Malaya) degree in 1977. This achievement was a turning point in my life, as I entered a field that required knowledge, empathy, and resilience. With newfound confidence, I was eager to begin my journey as a medical professional, prepared to make a difference in the lives of others. As I entered the field of medicine, I recognized that each patient encounter was not only a chance to apply my skills but also an opportunity for learning and personal growth. I embraced the challenges ahead, driven by a commitment to serve and heal those in need.

In those days, new medical graduates had to start internships right after their final exams due to a doctor shortage. Intern salaries in our class increased from RM650 to RM825 after our collective protest for higher pay. Later, they were revised upwards again until finally reaching

RM1165. This was a crucial moment in our journey, highlighting the importance of unity and advocacy in medicine. With each experience, we grew not only as clinicians but also as advocates for change within the healthcare system. During our internships, we realized the importance of tackling systemic issues that impacted both us and our patients. This newfound resilience spurred us to engage more actively in discussions about healthcare policies and their impact on our communities.

After a year as an intern at University Hospital Kuala Lumpur, I was able to register with the Malaysian Medical Council and obtained my medical license. This license is sometimes called a "license to kill," but I am dedicated to following the Hippocratic Oath, which emphasizes the importance of not causing harm. Equipped with my medical license, I felt a profound sense of responsibility to uphold the values associated with it. Every patient I meet serves as a reminder of the trust they place in healthcare professionals and the profound impact our decisions can have on their lives.

After graduating from the University of Malaya, my classmates and I managed to stay in touch and met up regularly using social media platforms like Facebook and WhatsApp messenger. We've built strong friendships since medical school, meeting every five years at first, but now we reunite annually. These gatherings are a valued tradition where we share experiences and support each other in the medical field. Each reunion not only strengthens our bonds but also reinforces our commitment to the ethical principles that guide our practice.

Our last reunion was held in Ipoh in 2022. We reminisced about old times while also discussing advancements in medicine and the challenges we faced in our respective careers. As we anticipate our upcoming gathering, a thrilling sense of excitement fills the air as we prepare to reconnect and exchange the new stories that life's journey has gifted us. It is these moments of connection that genuinely enhance our professional lives and highlight the significance of community in our field. The anticipation of laughter, shared experiences, and collaborative discussions brings a sense of warmth that we all cherish. We look forward to sharing not only our successes but also the lessons learned from our struggles. Each reunion strengthens our bonds and inspires us to continue striving for excellence in our endeavors.

THIS WORLD IS NOT OUR HOME

This world is not our home,
we are just passing through,
whatever good we can do,
now is the time to do,
we bring nothing when we come,
we take nothing when we go,
Godliness with contentment,
is the way to go,
whatever is noble,
whatever is true,
whatever is lovely,
whatever is good,
this we will do,
whatever is praiseworthy,
whatever is pure,
meditate more and more.

drandrewcskoh.com/poems

Chapter 4
Internship

"I have sometimes sat alone here of an evening, listening, until I have made the echoes out to be the echoes of all the footsteps that are coming by and by into our lives."

– A Tale of Two Cities, Charles Dickens.

In July 1977, my journey took me to University Hospital Kuala Lumpur, now University of Malaya Medical Centre (UMMC), where I began a one-year houseman (internship) as part of its compulsory prerequisite phase for fresh medical graduates registering with Malaysian Medical Council as practitioners. The experience consisted of two six-month rotations in Internal Medicine followed by Obstetrics & Gynecology. I experienced long hours and intense learning, but this time strengthened my commitment to the medical profession. Each day was filled with new cases, unforgettable lessons, and the opportunity to work alongside dedicated mentors who influenced my approach to patient care. The camaraderie among the housemen fostered a sense of teamwork that made even the toughest days bearable. During my rotations, I developed my clinical skills and confidence, shaping the doctor I would become. I learned to navigate the complexities of patient interactions and decision-making processes, which are essential in providing quality care. These experiences enhanced my medical knowledge and strengthened my commitment to serving the community and advocating for my patients. As I progressed through my training, I found that each challenge pushed me to grow both personally and professionally. This journey has deepened my understanding of the profound impact that compassionate care can have on individuals and their families.

INTERNSHIP

My accommodation was provided for free at the intern's quarters on the 14th floor, which made my on-call duties easier. At that time, my finances were limited, as I only had one hundred Malaysian ringgits in my bank account. It was truly a time filled with many ups and downs, reflecting Charles Dickens' words: "It was the best of times, it was the worst of times." Despite the financial strain, I found solace in the supportive network of fellow interns who shared similar experiences. Together, we forged friendships that helped us navigate the challenges of our demanding roles.

We often gathered in the common area to share stories and strategies, which lightened the weight of our responsibilities. These connections not only made the tough days more bearable but also enriched my overall internship experience.

When I was a medical student, I had to rely on a simple motorbike to get around. However, this meant that I would get wet if it rained, and I was at risk in case of accidents. I sold my old motorbike and bought a used Renault car for RM 1000. At first, it had some mechanical problems, but I later exchanged it for a dependable two-door Toyota Corolla sedan that rarely had breakdowns. This car was a worthwhile investment at RM 4000. Having reliable transportation made a significant difference in managing my daily responsibilities. It helped me concentrate on my internship instead of worrying about transportation.

With my newfound mobility, I felt an increased sense of independence and confidence in tackling my commitments. As I drove through the busy streets, I could focus on my personal growth and work without worrying about transportation issues. This newfound freedom allowed me to explore more opportunities, both within my internship and beyond. I could easily reach places without the stress of public transport.

INTERNAL MEDICINE

I began my Internal Medicine journey on Ward 13 of the University Hospital. There, I provided care for 28 patients under the supervision of a medical officer, lecturer, and professor. I had to do "Cinderella Call" duty every night from 12 midnight to 8 a.m. for my ward. This means that I had to be back by 12 midnight every day to be "on call" for my patients in ward 13.

Although challenging and restrictive, this experience showcased just how demanding medical careers can be. The distinctive challenges required my unwavering dedication and commitment! Every night brought a new set of circumstances that tested my resilience and adaptability. Yet, the opportunity to help those in need made every moment worthwhile. As I navigated through the exhaustion, each genuine smile of gratitude from my patients fueled my determination to keep going. In those moments, I realized that despite the long hours and sacrifices, my passion for medicine was my guiding light.

The Internal Medicine internship presented an incredible challenge. I begin my day with breakfast at the hospital cafeteria. Then, I quickly visit each patient to get to know them better. I learn their names, their preliminary diagnoses, test results, treatment plans, and any new admissions. At 10 am, the medical officer and lecturer started the daily ward rounds, which usually lasted for several hours. After that, I documented new cases, performed procedures, and reviewed test reports until late afternoon. Then, I handed over my responsibilities to the next houseman on call. As I wrapped up my day, I couldn't help but reflect on the diverse experiences and challenges each patient brought. It was in those moments that I felt a true sense of purpose in my role. Each case taught me something new, deepening my understanding and compassion for those in need. I looked forward to returning the next day, ready to embrace whatever challenges lay ahead.

One of the highlights of my Internal Medicine career was participating in weekly Professorial grand teaching ward rounds. Presenting each patient comprehensively to the Professor was a meticulous and extensive process that entailed involvement. Although these rounds took longer than other forms of medical learning, experiences gained proved invaluable. Discussing complex cases with experienced mentors improved my clinical reasoning and created a collaborative learning environment. Each round increased my appreciation for patient care and the value of teamwork in medicine. The deep interactions and shared knowledge fostered a sense of camaraderie among us as we navigated challenging cases together. This camaraderie not only enhanced our medical skills but also solidified friendships that would last throughout our careers.

There was a remarkable patient in Ward 13 who was a local celebrity radio DJ. She had a comforting voice and played emotional songs on the national radio from 11 pm to midnight every night. Due to her relationship with my professor, I gave her special treatment that made her stay as memorable as possible. I dedicated extra time to her, listening to her stories and learning about her experiences in the industry, which helped create a bond that went beyond the typical doctor-patient relationship. Our connection lifted her spirits in the hospital and motivated me to care for patients with empathy and compassion. As she recovered, her laughter filled the ward, bringing joy to staff and other patients. It was a reminder of the profound impact that genuine human connection can have on healing and resilience.

OBSTETRICS AND GYNAECOLOGY

Obstetricians and Gynaecologists play an essential role in healthcare delivery. Their expertise ensures women's physical well-being during pregnancy and childbirth and addresses broader health issues throughout their lives. By fostering strong relationships with their patients, they can better support their emotional and psychological needs as well. This holistic approach not only enhances the patient experience but also promotes overall health outcomes. As a result, many women feel empowered to make informed decisions about their care and future.

Obstetrics and Gynaecology provided me with an entirely unique set of experiences during the second half of my internship. Here, there was no "Cinderella Call duty," giving me more freedom once my daily duties had been completed. The patient's history-taking process was brief and concise. Lecturers and professors appeared to show less interest in comprehensive patient histories. Instead, there was a stronger emphasis on immediate clinical skills and hands-on practice. This shift allowed me to build confidence and develop my competencies in a fast-paced environment. I found myself enjoying the practical aspects of patient care, as I could apply my knowledge in real-time situations. This hands-on experience not only solidified my understanding but also sparked a deeper passion for the field of medicine.

Obstetrics and Gynaecology taught me invaluable practical skills for delivering babies and assisting in obstetric procedures. I witnessed both sad and comical events, including the tragic sudden death of a clerk from a rare fat embolism. Another patient experienced a life-threatening postpartum haemorrhage that required my professor to perform bilateral internal iliac artery ligations to save her. These experiences highlighted the unpredictability of medicine and the critical need for swift, effective interventions. They also reinforced my commitment to lifelong learning and the importance of staying abreast of advancements in medical techniques. Each day in the hospital presented a new set of challenges that tested my resilience and adaptability. These experiences made me more determined to positively impact the field and support patients in their vulnerable moments.

My most devastating memory is the tragic MH 653 air crash on December 4, 1977. It claimed the life of Professor I.S. Puvan. He was a remarkable Obstetrics and Gynaecology professor, known for his kindness, excellent bedside manner, and generous spirit. He once generously handed over RM 20 to a midwife, enabling her to buy a fulfilling dinner for the entire night shift team! I will never forget such a painful loss. His contributions to the field and the lives he touched continue to resonate with those who knew him. His absence highlights the fragility of life and the need to cherish our loved ones. As I reflect on his legacy, it's essential to honor his memory by nurturing kindness in my own life. Each small act can create ripples of positivity, just as he did.

Working in the labour ward was both exciting and unpredictable, with patients arriving during late hours. The way patients reacted to pain varied widely, from loud screams to a more Stoic display of endurance. Patients with low pain threshold are very distressed when in labour, and they need more sedation and analgesia. Patients with high pain threshold tolerate labour pain very well and do not require a lot of sedation and analgesia. This variability in pain perception emphasizes the importance of personalized care in the labour ward. Understanding each patient's unique threshold and response can lead to more effective pain management strategies. Additionally, effective communication between healthcare providers and patients is crucial in assessing pain levels and adjusting treatment plans accordingly. Creating a trusting environment allows medical staff to meet each patient's unique needs, improving their birthing experience.

I learned from experienced midwives the art of communicating during labour. Here is an example. The Indian word for breathe is "muchu". The Indian word for push is "muku". When an Indian patient is in labour, the houseman must say "muchu" (breathe) when a contraction stops. But when a contraction starts, the houseman must say "muku" (push).

One disaster occurred when a houseman reversed these two commands when attending to an Indian patient in labour. The patient became increasingly confused and anxious, leading to a chaotic situation in the delivery room. This incident highlighted the critical importance of clear communication and cultural understanding in medical practice. Such misunderstandings can have profound implications for patient care and outcomes. Healthcare professionals should undergo cultural training to be sensitive and effective with diverse patients.

I once learned the importance of staying silent after unintentionally disturbing a calm labor ward with a simple question. At that moment, I realized that sometimes, allowing space for silence can be more comforting than any words. It's essential to cultivate an environment where patients feel heard and understood, especially during vulnerable times. By fostering open communication and empathy, caregivers can build trust and improve the overall well-being of their patients. This approach not only enhances patient satisfaction but also contributes to better health outcomes in the long run. In these sensitive settings, every interaction counts, and the power of a compassionate presence cannot be overstated. Ultimately, it is through active listening and genuine care that we create a healing atmosphere for those in need.

MARRIAGE

On August 31st 1977, I married my wife who was studying Dentistry at the University of Malaya. We resided together after our marriage at houseman's quarters to begin a new journey together. As we settled into our lives, the challenges of balancing work and personal commitments began to shape our bond. Through each trial, our mutual support and understanding grew, laying a strong foundation for our marriage. We learned to communicate openly, finding comfort in the shared experiences that life presented. This commitment strengthened our relationship and created a strong partnership that lasted through the years. Over time, we grew to appreciate each other's strengths and quirks, making our daily routines feel special. Each moment, whether mundane or extraordinary, became a cherished memory in the tapestry of our lives together. We learned that even small acts of kindness can greatly strengthen our bond through life's challenges. With every laugh and tear, our love deepened, weaving us closer together in ways we never anticipated.

Wedding

TIME

One year, 365 days went by,
365 opportunities set aside,
One month, 30 days came
and went,
30 opportunities to connect
with friends.
One week, 7 days of good,
clean fun,
7 opportunities to save
enough,
One day, 24 hours to talk
with someone,
24 opportunities to walk as
one.
One hour, 60 minutes to
touch someone,
60 opportunities to share
heart-to-heart,
One minute, 60 seconds to
share WhatsApp,
60 opportunities to be a
friend.

drandrewcskoh.com/poems

Chapter 5
Taiping & Labuan

"Nothing that we do, is done in vain. I believe, with all my soul, that we shall see triumph."
– A Tale of Two Cities, Charles Dickens.

After finishing my internship at University Hospital, in 1978 I joined the Ministry of Health Malaysia. My first assignment was as a medical officer at Taiping District Hospital. The hospital offered essential medical services including medicine, surgery, obstetrics and gynecology, orthopedic, dentistry, oral surgery, and anesthesiology. During my time there, I gained invaluable hands-on experience and was able to develop my skills in various medical disciplines. Working with a dedicated team allowed me to engage with patients from various backgrounds, deepening my understanding of public health issues. I quickly learned the importance of communication and empathy in healthcare, which helped build trust with my patients. This pivotal experience established a strong foundation for my future pursuits in medicine and public health.

TAIPING EXPERIENCE

Taiping was the second-largest town in Perak, with a population of 245,182, known for attractions such as Taiping Zoo and Night Safari, Taiping Lake Gardens, and Maxwell Hill. My wife joined me on this tour of duty while also serving as government dentist at Taiping Hospital. We explored the town's history and culture, enhancing our personal and professional experiences. Together, we appreciated the unique blend of nature and community that Taiping offered, forging lasting memories along the way. My time in Taiping deepened my understanding of the vital role healthcare plays in community well-being. This experience strengthened my dedication to positively influencing others through medicine and public health.

Working at Taiping District Hospital was very different from my experience at University Hospital, which was mainly a teaching institution. Here, service was prioritized over training or continuous medical education. We were very short of medical staff. Even though the hospital had 15 medical officer posts, we only had 5 medical officers on staff. Nowadays, there's an oversupply of medical staff in this hospital, unlike when I worked there two decades earlier! The change in staffing has improved care delivery, emphasizing quality over quantity. It's fascinating to see how healthcare systems evolve over time in response to changing demands and challenges.

Taiping Hospital medical library facilities were severely lacking, making the place unsuitable for postgraduate education or research. Fortunately, the consultant physician at that time was academically inclined and passionate about teaching. He organized evening classes to help medical officers prepare for the MRCP (U.K.) Part 1 examination, which is an essential step in becoming an Internal Medicine Specialist. The classes became a beacon of knowledge and motivation, attracting many eager learners. As a result, the enthusiasm for learning fostered a culture of academic excellence within the hospital.

OUTPATIENT DEPARTMENT

For the initial six months of my tenure, I was assigned to the outpatient department, where patient volume was extreme. I used to see about 50 patients a day, making it difficult to take their history and perform physical exams. The department only had two medical officers instead of four to handle the large number of patients. This overwhelming workload necessitated efficient prioritization, and I quickly learned to streamline my approach without compromising care. The experience improved my skills in patient assessment and time management, preparing me well for my future practice. Despite the challenges, I found fulfillment in building rapport with patients and addressing their concerns effectively. Each interaction not only honed my clinical skills but also deepened my commitment to providing compassionate care.

At that time, the government was experiencing a severe shortage of medical practitioners. Fast-forward to 2020 and things have turned around. With an influx of graduates on the job market, internship posts are difficult to get compared with my time. In the past, new doctors were required to do two years compulsory government service. However, doctors are no longer required to do this nowadays. The shift has made the job market more competitive for new graduates, leading many to pursue extra qualifications to differentiate themselves. As a result, the healthcare landscape evolved rapidly, paving the way for innovative practices and improved patient care. This constant evolution necessitates continuous learning and adaptability among healthcare professionals. Ultimately, staying ahead in such a competitive environment is crucial for success and fulfillment in one's career.

MOBILE HEALTH CLINIC

After my time in the outpatient department, I was assigned to the mobile health clinic team. The clinic had one medical officer, one hospital assistant, one staff nurse, one dispenser, one attendant, and one driver. We provided outpatient services for five days a week, with Saturdays and Sundays being our rest days. We ventured beyond Taiping Hospital to provide outpatient services in the rural towns of Larut, Matang, and Selama districts. Our mission was to provide healthcare to those facing geographical or financial difficulties. Each day presented new challenges and opportunities to make a tangible difference in the lives of the patients we encountered. Our small team worked hard to provide quality medical care throughout the community. With each visit, we built trusting relationships, empowering patients to prioritize their health in ways they had previously thought impossible.

Our van transformed into a mobile clinic at each location. We stocked our van with appointments cards, case sheets, medications, syringes, needles, and other essentials. Our duty was to address and treat basic medical conditions like hypertension, diabetes, flu, and infections. Patients requiring hospitalization or special attention were referred directly to Taiping Hospital via referral letters. This seamless process ensured that our patients received continuity of care, fostering a sense of security and support. Each successful intervention not only improved individual health outcomes but also reinforced our commitment to serving the community's medical needs.

My daily schedule began at 7:30 am and concluded at 4 pm each clinic day. Grateful patients often gave us gifts like fish, crabs, prawns, fruits, and vegetables to show their appreciation. These tokens of gratitude brought us joy and strengthened our bond with the community we served. Such gestures made the long hours more rewarding and reminded us of the impact we had on their lives. Every day was filled with stories of resilience and hope, reinforcing the importance of our work. It felt truly fulfilling to know that we were making a difference, one patient at a time.

My wife and I regularly attended religious activities at the Taiping Gospel Hall church. We went for Sunday services and weekly Bible studies. The church was only a 30-minute drive away from our home. My parents also joined us in Taiping. Their presence brought us even closer as a family, sharing our faith and experiences together. We often organized family gatherings, where we enjoyed each other's company and deepened our spiritual connections. These gatherings became a cherished tradition, filled with laughter, shared meals, and heartfelt discussions about our beliefs. Through these moments, we found not just joy in each other's presence but also a strengthened commitment to our faith.

LABUAN TOUR OF DUTY

I changed my career path after spending a year in Taiping. I joined the Ministry of Defense as an army medical officer on a two-year contract through Malaysia's Ministry of Defense. I completed a month of army training at Kinrara Camp in Kuala Lumpur and became a Captain. I was appointed as a doctor at the army hospital in the Royal Malaysian Airforce Base on Labuan Island, East Malaysia. The experience was challenging yet rewarding, teaching me to adapt to military life while providing medical care to servicemen and their families. Living on Labuan Island helped me connect with the local culture and build lasting relationships.

In 1979, my wife and I flew on a C 130 military plane from Kuala Lumpur to Labuan. I was starting my first tour of duty as an officer at the Royal Malaysian Armed Forces Airbase in Labuan. Our journey lasted three and a half hours. We landed at an airbase near a military hospital, where we received free accommodation near the officers' quarters. My wife was also posted to the Labuan District Hospital as a dental officer. Settling into our new life, we quickly became acquainted with the other military families in the area. The atmosphere was vibrant, filled with camaraderie and a shared sense of purpose that made us feel at home. We often gathered for barbecues on the weekends, enjoying the warm weather and the company of our neighbors. These gatherings fostered lasting friendships that helped ease the transition into our new surroundings.

LABUAN MILITARY HOSPITAL

At RMAF Airbase Labuan, the military hospital was primarily designed for outpatient consultations and minor surgical procedures. I was responsible for managing the healthcare needs of army and air-force personnel and their families. I also conducted annual medical examinations for soldiers, army officers, airmen, and Airforce officers. Those who required hospitalization or major surgery were referred to nearby Labuan District Hospital. This experience helped me understand military medical protocols and the challenges service members face. Being part of this healthcare team improved my medical skills and instilled pride in serving those who protect our country.

My clinical workload was light, with about 20 patients to see daily. In the evenings, I played tennis, and at night, I socialized at the officers' mess, enjoying talks and affordable duty-free beer. In general, life in the army was nothing short of exhilarating. The reduced clinical duties gave ample opportunity for me to study, and I successfully passed the MRCP (U.K.) Part 1 Examination. This achievement opened doors for further specialization and professional development. With newfound confidence, I was ready to tackle the next challenges that lay ahead in my medical career.

At work, I wear a Captain's uniform. This means that lower-ranking personnel salute me and address me as "sir" multiple times each day. When I meet senior officers, we exchange salutes as well. Discipline in the military is taken very seriously as it could mean life or death in a war. This environment of respect and hierarchy instills a profound sense of responsibility within me. I understand that my actions and decisions can significantly impact both my team and the patients we serve. Every choice I make is a reflection of the values instilled in me through rigorous training and experience. This awareness drives me to constantly strive for excellence in every task I undertake.

LABUAN HOSPITAL

Because I had some free time in the army, I volunteered at the government-run Labuan District Hospital in Malaysia. I was privileged to assist a doctor friend at Labuan Hospital. This doctor was an outstanding surgeon performing appendectomy, hernia repairs, deliveries, Cesarean sections and more with ease. At that time, there were no qualified anesthetists, so hospital assistants gave general anesthesia despite lacking training. I saw the medical staff facing challenges while working hard to provide the best care in tough situations. This experience increased my respect for healthcare professionals and motivated me to pursue a career in medicine.

TRAGEDIES IN LABUAN

The unpredictable nature of life was clearly evident in Labuan. A close businessman friend faced insurmountable business challenges and tragically took his own life by hanging himself. The shockwaves of his death reverberated through the community, leaving many questioning how such despair could go unnoticed. It reminded me of the thin line between success and failure, motivating me to support mental health awareness. I realized that we must foster open conversations about mental health to prevent such tragedies in the future. This experience has strengthened my commitment to promoting comprehensive support systems in healthcare, so no one has to suffer in silence.

A deeply moving event has emerged in my mind. A pilot friend of mine died in a helicopter crash during a search and rescue mission in bad weather. This incident deeply affects me because he left behind a grieving wife and infant child. It is heart-wrenching to think about the family he left behind and the pain they now endure. These moments remind us to build a supportive community where everyone feels safe to share their struggles. We must also cherish every moment and express our love to those around us, for life is unpredictably fragile. In honoring his memory, I strive to be a better friend and a source of strength for those in need.

NOT WHAT BUT WHO YOU KNOW

As I spent my time in Labuan, the power of connections was ever present. My cousin worked as an airman at Labuan RMAF airbase and had been unsuccessfully applying for scholarships over many years. When I told a Major in the air force about our family connection, my cousin quickly got a scholarship to study aeronautical engineering in America! This remarkable turnaround was truly astounding given his longstanding and unsuccessful efforts at getting funding. It was a clear testament to the weight of relationships and the unexpected doors they can open. Seeing that transformation inspired me to build my own network, realizing that who you know can be just as important as what you know. I started connecting with professionals, attending workshops, and having conversations to create future opportunities. This proactive approach broadened my knowledge and connected me with potential mentors for my academic and career path.

IT'S A SMALL WORLD

"The world is a small place" came alive when I met someone in Labuan who recognized me but could not remember where we had met. During our conversations, it became evident that this person had actually been my MES scout master in Tanjong Malim. He was currently serving as an Admiral at Royal Malaysian Navy Base in Labuan. It has reinforced my belief that we can unexpectedly meet familiar people in faraway locations. This chance encounter serves as a reminder of the intricate web of relationships that we weave throughout our lives. It's fascinating how these moments can spark memories and connections that we thought were long forgotten. Reflecting on this encounter, I couldn't help but smile at the serendipity of it all. I realized how important it is to cherish our bonds, as they often come back to us unexpectedly.

A TRULY VALUABLE EXPERIENCE

My tenure in the army proved to be invaluable, offering respite from city life's hectic pace. I had the honor of attending a magnificent annual regimental night at my officer's mess. It was a special event where officers wore their full regimental attire and followed strict protocols. We had a delicious multi-course meal and received impeccable service from the staff. Additionally, I learned the proper use of cutlery and protocols, allowing me to handle formal occasions gracefully. The camaraderie among the officers created a warm and welcoming atmosphere that made the evening even more memorable. As the night progressed, stories and laughter filled the room, forging bonds that would last a lifetime. The evening culminated in a heartfelt toast, celebrating not only our achievements but also the enduring friendships we had formed. As we raised our glasses, I couldn't help but feel grateful for this unique experience that brought us all together.

LABUAN'S DUTY-FREE PERKS

Labuan was a tax-free port during this period. This has greatly reduced the cost of electronic and electrical goods in Labuan. Imported cars were available at substantial discounts thanks to duty exemptions. Many military officers purchased costly vehicles during their deployments, planning to return with them after their service. I bought a Honda Accord and a Nissan 120Y car at prices much lower than those in West Malaysia as they were duty free. I sent the cars home on a Navy ship when my tour ended! It was a practical decision that allowed me to save a significant amount of money. These vehicles served me well for years, reminding me of my unique experiences in Labuan. Throughout the ups and downs of civilian life, those cars reminded me of the friends I made and the adventures we had together. Each drive was a journey down memory lane, reminding me of the determination and camaraderie we developed during our time in service.

A TIME FOR EVERYTHING

A time for everything,
A time for every activity under heavens,
A time to be born, a time to die,
A time to plant, a time to uproot,
A time to kill, a time to heal,
A time to tear down, a time to build.
A time to weep, a time to laugh,
A time to mourn, a time to dance,
A time to scatter stones, a time to gather them,
A time to embrace, a time to refrain from embracing.
A time to search, a time to give up,
A time to keep, a time to throw away,
A time to tear, a time to mend.
A time to be silent, a time to speak,
A time to love, a time to hate,
A time for war, a time for peace.

Ecclesiates 3:1-8

Chapter 6

Kuala Lumpur, London & Teluk Intan

"He knew enough of the world to know that there is nothing in it better than the faithful service of the heart."
– A Tale of Two Cities, Charles Dickens.

After serving my military obligation in Labuan, I said goodbye to my Captain title and returned to civilian life. I began working as a medical officer at University Hospital Kuala Lumpur. Joining their Department of Internal Medicine was both exciting and challenging. Each day presented new cases and learning opportunities that pushed me to grow as a physician. My passion for helping others deepened as I forged connections with patients and colleagues alike. The diverse experiences I encountered in the hospital shaped my understanding of healthcare and empathy. I quickly realized that the journey of healing is just as important as the diagnosis itself.

After three years away from academic medicine, I realized I needed time and guidance to regain my footing and update my knowledge. With sufficient guidance and an accommodating environment at hand, I quickly returned to routine. This resurgence not only reignited my enthusiasm for medicine but also strengthened my commitment to serving others. Embracing the challenges once again, I felt revitalized and prepared to make a meaningful impact in the lives of my future patients. I developed a deeper understanding of compassion and empathy, qualities that are essential in patient care. Each interaction reminded me of the privilege it is to be part of someone's healing journey.

EXPANDING MY HORIZONS

Working at a teaching hospital was essential to my postgraduate training and accreditation in Internal Medicine. University Hospital's medical library offered me access to an abundance of resources. During this time, I encountered a variety of medical cases, gave presentations, did research, and published articles in medical journals. I also formed close relationships with Cardiology and Neurology Professors who saw me as their protégé. Their mentorship not only enhanced my clinical skills but also deepened my understanding of complex patient care. This experience confirmed my commitment to a career in Internal Medicine, allowing me to positively impact patients' lives.

My wife worked at the government dental clinic on Bangsar Road in Kuala Lumpur while we lived in a rented house in Taman Seputeh. Our family grew with the birth of our first son at University Hospital, and our parents came to help care for him. Alongside my medical duties and responsibilities, we attended the First Baptist Church in Taman Jaya, Petaling Jaya. The senior pastor of this church delivered impactful sermons with altar calls every Sundays. Community and spiritual connections enriched our lives and offered strong support during our early parenting. Our faith helped us stay grounded and resilient while facing work and family challenges. As our son grew, we found joy in participating in church activities and fostering friendships with other families. These connections became a source of encouragement, reminding us that we were never alone in this journey.

LONDON

Following my two-year residency at University Hospital, I took off for London to take my MRCP (U.K.) Part 2, the Examination for Internal Medicine Specialists. While in London, I worked as a locum Senior House Officer at St. Giles Hospital to gain work experience, but I encountered the high tax rates in the United Kingdom. Adjusting to the cost of living was tough, but it helped me manage my finances and budget more effectively. The chance to learn in a new environment greatly enhanced my professional skills and personal growth, despite the challenges.

This enabled me to gain exposure to the unique clinical practices in the United Kingdom. Collaborating with a diverse team of healthcare professionals expanded my view on patient care. This experience ultimately solidified my passion for internal medicine and reinforced my commitment to pursuing a career in this field. I now feel more equipped to tackle the complexities of healthcare, armed with the knowledge and skills I have acquired. I'm excited to continue this journey and make a positive impact on my future patients' lives.

On weekends, I visited a relative in London and explored nearby tourist spots. I participated in day trips to border towns in France organized by the hospital staff. These excursions gave me a break from my studies and helped me connect with colleagues more casually. Experiencing different cultures and perspectives further enriched my understanding of patient care and the importance of compassion in medicine. Sharing stories with my colleagues strengthened our relationships and highlighted the importance of teamwork in healthcare. Each interaction reinforced my commitment to serving patients with empathy and a well-rounded perspective.

EXPERIENCING ROMANS 8:28

The MRCP Part 2 examination consisted of both a theory module and a practical module, separated by several weeks. All theory modules must be successfully completed before progressing to the practical module. A trade war between Malaysia and Britain led to Malaysian candidates facing a higher failure rate in their qualification exams. This unexpected challenge prompted us to seek additional resources and support, fostering a collaborative spirit among the candidates. As we navigated these obstacles together, our resilience and determination only grew stronger. In the face of adversity, we learned the true importance of unity and perseverance within our group. This experience not only prepared us for the exams but also forged lasting friendships and a deeper sense of purpose.

By the grace of God, I successfully passed both the theoretical and practical modules on my first attempt and received the MRCP (U.K.) Diploma. It is a proof of Romans 8:28 that *"All things work together for good to those who love God, to those called according to His purpose."* I'm looking forward to the journey ahead and facing challenges with teamwork and faith. With this newfound confidence, I am eager to embrace the next chapter of my career. Each step forward feels like a testament to our collective efforts and unwavering belief in our goals. As I embark on this new adventure, I am reminded of the importance of resilience and dedication. I'm excited to see how these lessons will impact my career and personal growth in the future.

MALAYSIA

Upon returning to Malaysia in 1983, I was assigned as a Physician at the General Hospital in Kuala Lumpur. This accomplishment has reaffirmed my belief that faith and hard work can lead to extraordinary outcomes. Unfortunately, during that time, I was bullied and discriminated against by my colleagues in the Department of Medicine. This mistreatment was mainly from a Senior Physician who showed racist behavior while criticizing my actions. I couldn't take the mistreatment any longer, so I left my government job and started my own medical practice in Kuala Kubu Bahru, Selangor. My wife also moved there and got a job as a dental surgeon in the government. Inaugurating my own practice was refreshing, allowing me to foster a positive atmosphere for my patients and team. Together, we worked to build a community-focused healthcare service that prioritized compassion and respect for everyone.

KKB

Life in Kuala Kubu Bahru (KKB), was more relaxed than in Kuala Lumpur. I worked as a general practitioner (GP), providing outpatient care. My family and I regularly attended services at the Gospel Hall in Kuala Kubu Bahru. The pastor there became a close friend of ours. We attended Bible studies and Sunday services together as a family. While we were there, our second child was born, so now we are a family of four living in a rented house. Our children greatly valued their grandparents and cherished their roles as grandparents. They would often visit, bringing joy and warmth to our home. Family gatherings became lively events filled with laughter, love, and shared memories.

TELUK INTAN

I moved from Kuala Kubu Bahru to Teluk Intan in 1984. I worked as a physician in a Specialist Center, providing both outpatient and inpatient services. My wife also joined me and worked in a Government Dental Clinic. We purchased our first home within walking distance to my workplace. My parents also relocated to join us. Life in Teluk Intan was a new adventure for our family, full of chances to explore the local culture and community. Over the years, we made countless memories that tied us closer together in this vibrant town. We enjoyed weekend markets and traditional festivals, immersing ourselves in the rich tapestry of local traditions. Each experience deepened our roots, making Teluk Intan feel like home in every sense of the word.

CONNECTION TO CHURCH

We looked for a local church where we could serve, grow spiritually, and connect with others. After careful consideration, we decided to become members of the Wesley Methodist Church in Teluk Intan. The pastor there was very spiritual and gave sermons every Sunday that changed our lives. We went to the church's Sunday services and also attended the weekly Bible studies led by him. Through these gatherings, we formed meaningful relationships with fellow members of the congregation, which enriched our community experience. The supportive network provided a sense of belonging that further intertwined our lives with the vibrant culture of Teluk Intan. During our church activities, we found outreach programs to help those in need in the local community. This hands-on experience deepened our faith and strengthened our commitment to positively impact those around us.

REDEDICATION TO CHRIST

At a Christmas dinner hosted by Wesley Methodist Church in 1985, the pastor gave a deeply moving sermon. Following his sermon, he extended an altar call for those wanting to rededicate themselves to Christ again. I answered his call and went forward for prayer at the altar. This was a pivotal moment in my spiritual journey. It strengthened my commitment and motivated me to develop a closer relationship with God through independent Bible studies. I began to explore scriptures that resonated with my heart and challenged my understanding of faith. This journey opened my eyes to new insights and deepened my connection with God, transforming my everyday life. I found myself seeking out fellowship with others who shared similar beliefs, engaging in discussions that enriched my understanding. Each gathering became an opportunity for growth, as we shared our experiences and encouraged one another on our spiritual paths.

Additionally, I took part in Wesley Methodist Church's Navigator 2:7 Bible Study Series over six months. I memorized Bible verses by utilizing verse cards and practicing regular repetition. I still remember several of them today. The process enhanced my understanding of Scripture and strengthened my commitment to apply its teachings in my daily life. This newfound dedication inspired me to look for ways to serve my community and put my faith into action.

CALEB GROUP & FGBMFI

I started a group called the Caleb Group at my home. We gathered every Monday evening from 7:30 to 9:30 p.m. This lasted about a year and led to significant personal and spiritual breakthroughs for me and the church community. The support and encouragement we provided each other fostered a deep sense of belonging and purpose. As a result, we were able to engage in various outreach projects that positively impacted those around us.

Additionally, I served on the committee of Full Gospel Businessmen's Fellowship International's (FGBMFI). We organized lunch meetings and dinner gatherings where non-Christian friends could listen to Christian professionals share their evangelistic testimonies. Those who responded to the altar calls were directed to local churches for further discipleship and follow-up. This effort not only strengthened our community ties but also opened up opportunities for meaningful conversations about faith. Seeing the positive changes in participants' lives strengthened my dedication to this mission and inspired me to find more ways to help.

MY PARENTS – TRULY A BLESSING

My parents' presence was an incredible boon in our lives. They played an invaluable role in caring for our children while we pursued careers. Their assistance was crucial, especially when we depended on Indonesian maids as domestic helpers. They usually had two-year contracts. As our children grew close to them, saying goodbye was often a mix of emotions. It was difficult for the kids to understand why these caregivers had to leave after forming such strong bonds. Yet, my parents always stepped in to provide the steady love and support that made the transitions easier for everyone. Their presence reminded us that family could take many forms, and the lessons of love and care transcended temporary goodbyes. Each farewell became a part of our journey, teaching us about resilience and the importance of cherishing every moment together.

My parents became Christians because of our influence. Although they have passed away because of old age, I find solace in knowing that we will meet again in heaven. Their faith remains a guiding light in my life, reminding me to hold onto hope and love even in their absence. Each day, I carry their lessons in my heart, striving to honor their memories through acts of kindness and compassion. As I navigate the challenges of life, their spirit encourages me to embrace every opportunity for growth and connection. I often reflect on the beautiful moments we shared, which continue to inspire me to live fully and meaningfully. In these reflections, I draw strength from their laughter and wisdom, allowing their legacy to shape my path forward. Each memory becomes a thread woven into the tapestry of my life, reminding me of the love that transcends both time and space.

Parents, wife, and sons

COVID 19

2019 ended with a cry,
2020 full of surprise,
Chained to our homes by
the Covid guy.
Economies collapsing left
and right,
Hoteliers crying out with a
sigh,
Food Panda laughing to
the bank,
Grab Food flourishing with
a bang!
Internet shoppers
shopping in style,
2020 ended with another
cry,
For 2021 to vaccinate the
Covid guy.

andrewcskoh.com/poems

Chapter 7

Malaysia & New Zealand

"A wonderful fact to reflect upon, that every human creature is constituted to be that profound secret and mystery to every other."

A Tale of Two Cities, Charles Dickens.

In 1986, I relocated once more, leaving Telok Intan and joining the Ipoh Specialist Center (ISC) as a Physician. After I moved to Ipoh and bought a house, my family also moved there. In the same year, my third son was born at the Ipoh Specialist Centre. The arrival of my son brought great joy to our family, and we quickly adjusted to life in Ipoh. At ISC, I found joy in caring for the community while managing family life. The support from my colleagues at ISC made the transition easier and created a strong sense of camaraderie. Balancing work and family became a rewarding challenge, and I cherished every moment spent with my growing children. As they explored the world around them, their laughter filled our home with warmth and happiness. Each day was a new adventure, and I felt grateful for the love that surrounded us.

CHALLENGING TIMES AT SCHOOL

While living in Ipoh, my children attended Anglo-Chinese School (ACS). One of my sons had a challenging time in Primary 1 because he was very shy and introverted. He would often cry and refuse to go to school. As a result of this situation, he needed my late father's constant companionship, even staying during breaks, so he could buy food from the canteen. Additionally, he was frequently bullied by a Punjabi student in class and his teacher expressed concerns regarding his progress. This situation deeply worried me, as I wanted him to adapt and thrive in his new environment. I decided to step in, speak with his teacher, and explore ways to help him gain confidence and feel more secure in school.

One day, my uncle from Bidor visited ACS school to meet up with my father. Hearing about my son's problem, he met up with my son's teacher, who was also from Bidor. After this conversation, the teacher paid special attention and helped my son overcome his learning difficulties. Soon after this, a classmate befriended my son and from that day forward they were close friends. He helped my son to overcome his introversion and shyness. We thank God that this amazing friend came into my son's life in his time of need.

I was saddened when this boy tragically passed away due to a fire accident in 2019. The loss was devastating for our family and for my son, who had formed such a deep bond with him. Amid our grief, we found comfort in the cherished memories and the lessons of kindness and friendship that will always stay with us. Though the pain of his absence lingers, we strive to honor his memory by spreading the same warmth and support he offered to my son. It reminds us to appreciate every moment and to be there for others in need, just as he was for us.

GROWING DEEPER IN FAITH

Spiritually, our journey continued when the pastor from Teluk Intan moved on to Wesley Methodist Church in Ipoh. Following him, we joined that church, which offered more opportunities for Bible studies. I attended Bible seminars every six weeks led by a gifted teacher from Singapore, covering all books from Genesis to Revelation. I bought his books, audiotapes, and CD ROMs to support him and to help deepen my faith and knowledge.

These resources became invaluable tools in my spiritual growth, enriching my understanding of scripture and the teachings of Christ. As I engaged more deeply in these studies, I discovered a renewed sense of purpose and a stronger connection to my faith community. This sense of belonging encouraged me to get more involved in church activities and build meaningful relationships with other members. Each new connection reinforced my commitment to living out my faith in practical ways, fostering both personal and communal growth.

BROTHER PAUL TAN

Brother Paul Tan was an extraordinary Bible teacher and former Principal of Tung Ling Bible Seminary in Singapore. His late father was a co-worker with Watchman Nee. Brother Paul displayed exceptional teaching abilities rooted in verse-by-verse exegesis with historical context, biblical exposition, and other approaches. His passion for scripture shone through in every lesson, engaging his students and fostering a love for the Word. Under his guidance, many found their calling in ministry and deepened their understanding of Christian theology. His legacy continues to inspire future generations of leaders and scholars in the faith. The impact of his mentorship is felt not only in the classrooms but also in the hearts of those he taught.

Under Brother Paul's guidance, I embarked on an incredible journey through every book of the Bible, from Genesis to Revelation, exploring the fullness of God's counsel. I was deeply inspired by his teaching. He had a unique ability to make scriptures come alive. I admired his anointing, Biblical knowledge, communication skills, and spiritual gifts. He was also profoundly devoted to his Word and never wavered in his commitment. His unwavering faith had a profound impact on all who listened. I found myself growing in knowledge and spirit, eager to apply what I've learned in my daily life. With each gathering, I felt a deeper connection to my faith and a renewed sense of purpose. It was inspiring to witness how his teachings encouraged others to embark on their own spiritual journeys.

Brother Paul became my closest friend, a valuable role model, and a trusted guide. His passing was sad, but his legacy motivated me to study full-time at a Bible college. Every lesson I learned there further solidified my commitment to living a life of service and compassion. I knew that through sharing Brother Paul's wisdom, I could help others find their own path to fulfillment and connection. I started to understand spirituality and how to use it in daily life as I explored the teachings. This new purpose brought me peace and encouragement to explore my faith.

PUBLIC LISTING OF ISC

I advanced my medical career with a visiting cardiology fellowship at Royal Northshore Hospital in Sydney in 1989 and 1991. While I was away, locums took over my responsibilities in Ipoh. Upon my return, I was eager to reintegrate into the community and share the knowledge I had gained.

In 1994, the Ipoh Specialist Centre, owned by a group of medical specialists, became a publicly traded company through a corporate takeover and was listed on Malaysia's Stock Exchange. This change improved the center's profile and expanded the services we can offer to our patients. I was excited about the opportunities this presented for improving healthcare in our community.

Shortly after the public listing, I left Ipoh Specialist Centre to establish my own independent cardiology clinic in Ipoh City Centre. This decision allowed me to provide more personalized care and cater specifically to the needs of my patients. Establishing my own clinic was challenging but rewarding, as I had to balance running a business with caring for patients. Through dedication and hard work, my clinic quickly gained a reputation for cardiology services within the community. As word of mouth spread, I began to attract patients from surrounding areas who were seeking cardiology service.

At the end of 1998, however, I sold my practice and moved with my wife and children to Auckland, New Zealand. This new chapter in our lives brought exciting opportunities and challenges.

1997 ASIAN FINANCIAL CRISIS

Working privately allowed me to earn much more than I did working for the government. In 1997, the Asian Financial Crisis severely impacted Malaysia, causing a sharp depreciation of its currency due to attacks from speculators and capital flight. Malaysia only recovered from this setback sometime around 1999. I saw how difficult it was for businesses and families to cope with the uncertain economy during this tough time. The resilience of the Malaysian people motivated me to adapt and explore new opportunities in New Zealand.

Share prices dropped quickly and unexpectedly, leaving investors to incur heavy losses and some even went bankrupt overnight! Property values also saw steep decreases, while cars were often sold at heavy discounts. I wasn't directly affected and did not sustain any financial loss during this financial meltdown. Rather, it enabled me to purchase my house in Ipoh at an incredible discount price! This fortunate turn of events allowed me to establish a stable and comfortable life for my family. Embracing this new chapter, I started to appreciate the beauty of my heritage as well as the exciting experiences that New Zealand had to offer.

BIBLE COLLEGE OF NEW ZEALAND

In 1999, I studied at Laidlaw Bible College in New Zealand for one year. I completed a Diploma of Graduate Theology and then a Postgraduate Diploma of Theological Studies at Laidlaw College. Before pursuing her graduate diploma, my wife studied counseling, showing her great dedication to her academic pursuits. My sons studied in Auckland before continuing at Otago University. This shared commitment to education fostered a strong intellectual environment in our family. Together, we navigated the challenges and triumphs of our respective studies, creating lasting memories along the way.

My two sons excelled in high school. Both of them achieved the prestigious title of Dux Scholars at Mount Albert Grammar School. Teachers were delighted with how well my boys represented the school by providing such outstanding students. Their success brought great renown and goodwill towards Mount Albert Grammar School as they fostered an environment conducive to learning. Their accomplishments inspired their peers and left a positive legacy for future students. We celebrated our children's hard work and dedication, making memories during this exciting time in our lives. As we shared laughter and stories, it became clear that these moments would be cherished forever. This milestone not only marked a culmination of their efforts but also the beginning of new adventures ahead.

At one of the "meet the teacher" sessions, one of my son's teachers asked, "*Have any more sons for us*?" To which I responded, "*Yes! I have one more*!"

My youngest son performed excellently at Glendene Primary School and later attended high school in Dunedin, where he excelled academically. He was honored with the prestigious title of Dux Scholar. I am grateful to God for my three intelligent sons. I thank Him daily for blessing our family with such remarkable minds. Each achievement fills my heart with pride, knowing the dedication and hard work that went into their success. As they continue to grow and tackle new challenges, I look forward to witnessing the incredible paths they will forge. Their determination and passion inspire me to be the best version of myself. Together, we will celebrate each milestone and embrace the journey ahead.

HONOR GOD AND HE WILL HONOR YOU

Studying in the Bible College was one of the greatest blessings in my life. I felt truly honoured to offer myself up as a living sacrifice for Jesus. On my first day of class, a teacher encouraged us to dedicate ourselves to Him and to make prayerful offerings throughout the year. He said that if we honour Him He will honor us back! This powerful message resonated deeply with me and became a guiding principle in my spiritual growth. I added prayer to my daily routine, asking for His guidance in all areas of my life. With each passing day, I found that my faith grew stronger and clearer, guiding me through challenges and uncertainties. I found that true fulfillment comes from helping others and sharing Christ's love in meaningful ways.

Bible College helped me improve my writing and research skills. I also learned how to use the library for self-learning and assignments.

Furthermore, it honed my ability to think critically, theologically, and logically. These are essential skills. They not only enhance my academic pursuits but also equip me to engage more effectively in ministry. As I continue this journey, I am excited to apply what I've learned to positively impact my community. The knowledge and skills I've gained will allow me to serve with greater compassion and understanding. I look forward to fostering deeper connections and facilitating meaningful conversations within my community. By sharing my experiences and insights, I hope to inspire others to join me in this mission. Together, we can build a more supportive and inclusive environment for everyone involved.

GRADUATION

My journey at Bible College was marked by both academic challenges and meaningful relationships with fellow students. Each module necessitated consistent participation in lectures, completion of assignments, and passing of examinations. I also valued the opportunity to build meaningful connections outside of the classroom. These relationships enriched my time at college and provided a support system that was invaluable during tough times. Upon graduating with dual degrees, I realized that the experiences and connections I made were just as valuable as the academic knowledge I acquired.

After an exhilarating three years in college, I proudly graduated and participated in the graduation ceremonies. As I walked across the stage to receive my diplomas, a wave of nostalgia enveloped me, reminding me of all the challenges I had overcome. With my family cheering from the audience, I felt a sense of accomplishment that not only marked the end of my academic journey, but also the beginning of a new chapter filled with endless possibilities. Stepping off the stage, I was filled with gratitude for everyone who had supported me along the way. Looking forward, I felt excited about the adventures and opportunities in my career.

TWO SAD INCIDENTS

Attending Bible College was a time of growth, but two tragic incidents affected our community. A student with depression sadly took his own life by inhaling carbon monoxide from his car in a closed garage. I was deeply saddened and shocked by this tragic event. The loss resonated throughout the campus, leaving behind a profound sense of grief and contemplation about mental health. We united as a community to support each other and highlighted the need to seek help in tough times.

The second incident hit even harder when the cherished principal of the Bible College passed away unexpectedly. Brian Harthaway's sudden death due to a heart attack while out for his morning jog was deeply mourned by the community of Laidlaw College. Just minutes into his run, he collapsed and passed away. Having completed his race here on earth, he is now at home with the Lord. May his soul rest in peace. His loss deeply affected the college, prompting a wave of grief and remembrance from students and faculty members. His commitment to fostering faith and character in his students will always be remembered by those he inspired. The memorial service held in his honor brought together the entire community, offering a space for shared memories and healing. As stories were exchanged, it became clear that his legacy would continue to impact lives for years to come.

A TRULY ENRICHING EXPERIENCE

At Bible College, I had a fulfilling experience both academically and spiritually. My professors were well-known Bible scholars and pastors who taught me about theology, exegesis, hermeneutics, spiritual growth, preaching, evangelism, Biblical texts, missions, and pastoral care. Each class pushed me to deepen my understanding and grow in my personal faith by actively engaging with the Scriptures. The friendships I formed with fellow students were invaluable and enriched our shared faith journey. Through late-night discussions and group studies, we challenged one another to think critically and live out our beliefs authentically. Those moments not only strengthened our bond but also prepared us for the challenges that lay ahead in ministry.

Students representing Malaysia, Singapore, Hong Kong, Taiwan, Korea, Indonesia, and the Fiji Islands were among our diverse student body. We went beyond studying in the classroom and got involved in Kelston Community Church (KCC). At KCC, we took part in outreach programs to engage with the local community and demonstrate our faith. These experiences highlighted the importance of service and compassion, strengthening our commitment to positively affect the world.

Kelston Community Church and Bible College hosted regular potluck dinners, which provided opportunities for fellowship and shared meals. These gatherings fostered a sense of belonging and allowed us to celebrate our diverse cultures through food and stories. They were a reminder that our differences enriched our community, bringing us closer together in unity and purpose. As we shared laughter and food, we also shared our hopes and challenges, creating deeper connections among us. This spirit of togetherness not only strengthened our bonds but also inspired us to continue serving others in our community.

However, one of the standout experiences during our time at Bible College was visiting a Marae in Auckland. Maraes are unique to New Zealand and serve as community meeting places for the Maori people. They consist of intricately carved Maori structures within enclosed enclosures, separated by fencing or gates. Our visit to the Marae let us experience Maori culture and traditions through welcoming ceremonies and insights into their history. This profound experience deepened our appreciation for cultural diversity and reinforced our desire to build bridges between communities.

During our two-day stay on a Maori Marae, we explored its history and culture through traditional songs and dances and the Haka. Enjoying authentic "hangi" lunches and dinners offered us the chance to sample authentic Maori cuisine. We rested on separate floor mattresses in the communal hall during the night. We sang Christian hymns and shared testimonies before falling asleep. Sometimes, we were woken up by loud snores from some participants! Despite the interruptions, the camaraderie and shared experiences made for great memories. Every morning, we would wake up early to enjoy the beautiful sunrises over the hills, feeling thankful for our warm community.

The Asian Christian Fellowship was formed among the influential Asian community at our college, consisting of students from Malaysia, Singapore, Hong Kong, China, Taiwan, Japan, and Korea. Here, I noticed that Japanese, and Korean students often struggled with their assignments due to poor command of English. Weekly lunch meetings and monthly potluck dinners further cemented our bonds as one community. These gatherings offered support and a chance to celebrate our diverse cultures through food and tradition. Sharing our stories helped us appreciate our differences and find common ground in our faith and goals.

One notable member of our fellowship was a gifted Japanese student who also happened to be a professional hairdresser. She generously shared her expertise, offering invaluable hairdressing tips for both men and women as she showcased her talent. I can vouch that having my hair cut by her was one of the finest experiences of my life! Additionally, our diverse community offered classes in car maintenance and culinary arts where talented students would share their expertise. These hands-on experiences enhanced our skills and strengthened our relationships as we learned from one another. As we gathered in the workshop or kitchen, laughter echoed through the room, creating lasting memories that transcended our differences.

SOJOURN IN WELLINGTON

After Bible College, I worked for two years as a senior fellow of Internal medicine and cardiology in Wellington. I had to be separated from my wife and youngest son for this endeavor. My two older sons went to Otago University in Dunedin. One studied medicine, and the other studied dentistry. The distance was challenging, but it allowed me to focus on my career while supporting my family from afar. During this time, I often reflected on the importance of family and the sacrifices we make for our aspirations. Despite the challenges, I found comfort in the knowledge that my efforts would ultimately lead to a better life for all of us. Each milestone they achieved felt like a shared victory, strengthening our bond even across the miles.

I worked at Masterton Hospital and Wellington Hospital during this period. I served on the committee of the New Zealand Overseas Trained Doctor's Association. This organization helped overseas-trained doctors whose qualifications weren't recognized by the Medical Council, preventing them from practicing in New Zealand. Through advocacy and support, we aimed to navigate the complexities of the medical system together. It was incredibly rewarding to witness talented individuals overcome barriers and contribute to the healthcare community.

Many of our members overcame these challenges by transitioning to temporary work like taxi driving, real estate, or nursing. Many members obtained provisional registration and hospital positions by collaborating, lobbying politicians, and engaging with the Medical Council. Some even chose to move to Australia, where the process of obtaining registration and positions was easier. Their resilience and determination not only opened doors for themselves but also inspired others in similar situations. As a community, we witnessed the power of unity and support in transforming lives and creating a brighter future for everyone.

GOD'S HAND OF PROVISION

I could only practice medicine in New Zealand because of God's intervention. Foreign graduates faced challenges registering as doctors in New Zealand, and my qualifications were initially rejected by the

Medical Council. However, after persistent effort and countless prayers, I received the guidance I needed to navigate the complex regulations. It became clear that with faith and perseverance, even the most daunting obstacles could be overcome, resulting in a rewarding career in medicine.

I prayed and fasted sincerely, and God helped me connect with a Medicine Professor from Wellington University. He endorsed me, and I got provisional registration to practice medicine in New Zealand for two years. However, I felt that New Zealand was not my final destination, so I returned home after my contract ended. Back in my homeland, I reflected on my journey and the experiences that had shaped my aspirations. With renewed determination, I began exploring opportunities that would take me to the next chapter of my medical career.

RECOLLECTION OF 9/11

I clearly remember the morning of September 11, 2001, when the world was shaken by a terrorist attack. During breakfast in the doctor's lounge, I watched the news and saw a video of Flight 175 hitting one of the Twin Towers in New York. This deeply affected me and my colleagues. Initially, it seemed like Hollywood fiction, but when a newsreader confirmed it was real, I was deeply shocked and upset. The gravity of the situation sank in as we realized the scale of the tragedy unfolding before our eyes. We gathered in front of the TV, trying to understand what was happening in the United States. As the day went on, stories of heroism and loss emerged, changing how we view vulnerability and resilience.

BACK TO IPOH

After five years living in New Zealand, my wife, my youngest son and I returned to Ipoh, Malaysia in 2003. Our two older sons remained behind to pursue their careers, one studying Medicine while the other Dentistry. The streets of Ipoh felt both familiar and new as we explored the busy markets and quiet neighborhoods. It was a bittersweet reunion, tinged with nostalgia and the realization of how much had changed during our time away. The colorful market stalls and delicious street food reminded me of my childhood. While walking through the busy streets, I felt both excited and nervous about reconnecting with our old life.

In Ipoh, I joined Perak Community Specialist Hospital as a Resident Cardiologist while also serving as a Visiting Cardiologist at KPJ Ipoh Specialist Hospital. Running a private medical practice included managing an outpatient clinic, performing cardiology procedures, handling interventional treatments, and addressing emergency cases. Constantly working and being available, combined with sleep disruptions and long-term radiation exposure, harmed my health and social life. Managing time is extremely important to avoid burnout. Taking periodic sabbatical leaves can be very helpful in providing necessary breaks to reset, recharge, and restore balance. My time at Bible college was crucial in implementing this strategy. It allowed me to step back from the chaos of everyday responsibilities and focus on spiritual growth and self-care. Engaging in reflective practices and building community during that time significantly improved my overall well-being.

A CALLING

As a doctor, I often received emergency calls at strange hours, including nights and weekends. It was more than just work or a profession for me. It felt like a divine calling and a passion. I missed important moments with my sons because of that. However, I made sure to share Bible stories with my youngest son every night before he went to sleep. These moments became precious rituals that strengthened our bond and instilled values I hoped would guide him through life. I wanted him to appreciate the importance of service and compassion, similar to what I learned as a doctor.

As my sons have grown into adults with their own families, they no longer feel as close to me as before. If I could go back in time, I would try harder to develop stronger connections. I have faith in God and look forward to building lasting relationships with my grandchildren. I cherish the opportunity to share my experiences and wisdom with them, hoping to create new traditions and memories together. With each passing day, I am reminded of the importance of nurturing these connections that truly enrich our lives. As I embark on this new chapter, I remain open to learning from them just as much as I hope they learn from me. Together, we can weave a vibrant tapestry of love and understanding that spans generations.

MARKETPLACE SOUL-WINNER

I saw myself as a *"marketplace soul-winner."* I shared the Gospel with my patients whenever I could, using my office as a way to bring hope through God's word. I brought solace to patients by leading them in prayer. For those who were already Christians, I offered heartfelt prayers during visits. I aimed to create an environment where faith and healing intertwined seamlessly. My passion for my work and faith inspired me to positively affect everyone I met.

My family and I attended Holy Cross Lutheran Church in Ipoh. The sense of community and shared belief there provided a strong foundation for my spiritual journey. It was in this nurturing environment that I truly began to appreciate the power of connection through faith. Together, we engaged in various outreach programs that extended support to those in need. This experience strengthened our bonds and deepened my understanding of the impact of faith on people's lives.

I also enthusiastically attended weekly Bible seminars conducted by an anointed Pastor from Kuala Lumpur. He taught the Bible book by book from Genesis to Revelation, focusing on its interpretation and meaning. These sessions deepened my understanding of scripture and strengthened my faith in God. Every week, I departed feeling spiritually refreshed, integrating the teachings into my everyday life. I felt a deep bond with others on similar faith journeys, as we shared a desire for spiritual growth and support. We shared personal testimonies, prayed together, and celebrated the transformative power of God's word. This sense of community not only enhanced my faith but also fostered lasting friendships that continued to inspire me.

PILGRIMAGE

I had the incredible honor of accompanying this Pastor on two pilgrimages to the Holy Land in 2005 and 2019. As I visited the key spots described in the sacred texts, both trips truly brought Biblical passages to life. Pilgrimage sites included the Sea of Galilee, Mount Carmel, Bethlehem, Joppa, Mount of Olives, Western Wall, Shiloh, Temple Mount, City of David, Magdala, Capernaum, En Gedi, Via Dolorosa, Garden Tomb, Gethsemane, Church of Holy Sepulcher, Temple Institute, Hezekiah's Tunnel, and the Pool of Siloam among many others. Our pilgrimage experience ignited my passion for God's words.

Each location deepened my understanding of the scriptures and the historical significance of these sacred sites. The moments spent reflecting and praying in these holy places were truly transformative and reaffirmed my spiritual journey. The vibrant history and powerful presence of each site resonated deeply within me. This journey strengthened my faith and deepened my connection to the stories that have impacted many lives over time. Furthermore, I found myself more committed to living out those teachings in my daily life. This renewed commitment inspires me to share my experiences and insights to encourage others on their spiritual journeys.

TUNG LING

My wife and I pursued theological studies at Tung Ling Seminary in Ipoh over three years, attending evening courses taught by distinguished lecturers from Kuala Lumpur's Tung Ling Seminary. This six-week program ran daily from 6 pm to 10 pm and included lectures, workshops, assessments, and exams led by Tung Ling lecturers from Kuala Lumpur. The rigorous schedule allowed us to deeply engage with the subjects while balancing our personal and professional lives. Our time there enriched our understanding of theology and deepened our commitment to serving our community. As we immersed ourselves in the curriculum, we formed lasting friendships with fellow students who shared our passion for learning. Together, we created a supportive network that encouraged spiritual growth and collaboration beyond the classroom.

CONFERENCES

I attended local, regional, and international cardiology seminars and conferences for my continuing medical education. This is needed for the renewal of my annual medical practicing certificate. Through these seminars, I gained valuable insights into the latest advancements in cardiology and best practices in patient care. Each experience deepened my knowledge and strengthened my commitment to delivering excellent patient care. There is also an opportunity to tour the city after the conference. Exploring the local culture and sights allowed me to unwind and appreciate the regions I visited. These experiences not only enriched my professional development but also provided a refreshing perspective on my work. Over the years, I have travelled numerous countries around the world.

GOD'S CONSTANT FAITHFULNESS

Every year, we visit Dunedin in New Zealand, as well as Melbourne in Australia. We go there to see our children, daughters-in-law, grandsons, and granddaughters. Our family grew from two members in 1977 to fourteen in 2020. God's faithful presence has guided us through life's challenges. Through every joyful reunion and hurdle faced, we have witnessed the strength of our family's bond. It is in these moments of connection that we truly recognize the blessings bestowed upon us. As we gather around the table, laughter fills the air, echoing the love that binds us together. Each shared story and cherished memory reinforces the importance of family in our lives. In the warmth of our gatherings, we are reminded that no obstacle is insurmountable when supported by one another. Our collective hope and unwavering faith pave the way for brighter days ahead.

BOBBY

Bobby (an Alsatian-Mongrel mix) was my faithful companion when living in Ipoh. I brought him home as a puppy. From the moment he arrived, his playful spirit and boundless energy transformed our home into a place filled with joy. Every adventure we shared forged an unbreakable bond that I will forever hold close to my heart.

One day, a venomous cobra entered our property, and Bobby demonstrated remarkable bravery by barking at the intruder to prevent it from getting in. I immediately summoned the Fire-Rescue Squad for assistance, and they safely removed it. I will always be thankful to Bobby for his selfless act of courage! He showed a level of loyalty that deepened my appreciation for our companionship. Moments like these reinforced the deep connection we shared, reminding me of how fortunate I was to have him by my side. As the days went by, I made sure to give Bobby extra treats and affection to show my gratitude. Our bond only grew stronger, and I knew that together we could face any challenge that came our way.

Unfortunately, after nine years Bobby became old and fragile. One rainy day when I opened the gate, he suddenly bolted out of the house. I hoped he'd return later but didn't. For days my wife and I searched the neighborhood in vain and no sign of Bobby could be found anywhere. The emptiness in our home grew heavier with each passing moment. We clung to memories of his playful spirit, hoping that somehow he was safe and happy wherever he had wandered. As we called his name while walking through the streets, the distant laughter of children reminded us of the joy he once gave us. Every night, we kept the porch light on, hoping he would return, and we would see him coming down the path.

Three days later, I found him lying helplessly in a nearby field. I brought him home, cared for him but, tragically, Bobby peacefully passed away within days despite my best efforts. I laid him to rest in our compound. Although his death was painful, finding comfort in the fact that we were finally reunited helped ease the burden of guilt-laden memories that haunted me. As I placed the last handful of soil on his grave, I whispered promises to keep his memory alive. The bond we shared would forever remain etched in my heart, a testament to the love we had for each other. I often found myself reminiscing about the joyful moments we spent together, each memory a bittersweet reminder of his presence. In honoring his spirit, I pledged to share our story with others, hoping to inspire compassion and kindness toward all living beings.

Convocation

LOCKED DOWN

Locked down but
not out,
Knocked down but
not out!
Chained to the
house,
But not to the
ground.
Chained to iPad and
iMac,
Mind soared upon
high.
Covid-19 on the rise,
Vaccine arise and
shine!

andrewcskoh.com/
poems

Chapter 8
Nothing Short of a Miracle

"A dream, all a dream, that ends in nothing, and leaves the sleeper where he lay down, but I wish you to know that you inspired it."

– *A Tale of Two Cities, Charles Dickens.*

I was invited to a celebratory dinner at a renowned hotel on December 26, 2019, hosted by the committee members of the Ipoh Cardiovascular Society, a group of cardiologists. The atmosphere was filled with excitement as the evening promised engaging discussions and valuable networking opportunities. As I sat down, I felt grateful for the opportunity to connect with respected professionals. The table was beautifully set, and the aroma of exquisite dishes wafted through the air, enhancing the sense of anticipation. Conversations flowed easily as colleagues shared insights and experiences, deepening our connections in the field of cardiovascular health. The room was filled with laughter and camaraderie, creating a joyful celebration of our shared commitment to improving patient care. During the night, I reflected on how innovations in cardiology were changing our practices and improving patients' lives.

THE ACCIDENT

As I finished a nice dinner and got ready to leave, an accident would change my life forever. While I was walking out, I lost my footing and fell on the floor. I lost consciousness for some time. As I regained consciousness, I noticed my friends anxiously calling my name, their faces filled with concern. The surrounding chaos slowly came into focus, and I realized the gravity of what had just happened. I felt as though my head was the only part of me that existed. I could not figure out where the rest of my body was. Panic surged through me as I strained to move, struggling to understand the disconnection between my head and body.

I quickly began to sense that something was amiss. My body couldn't feel anything from the neck down. It was alarming and terrifying. I couldn't move my hands or feet and didn't have any sensation below my neck. I was told later on that this phenomenon is called spinal shock due to acute spinal cord compression. The doctors explained that it might take time for the feeling to return, but the uncertainty weighed heavily on my mind. As I lay there, I wondered if I would ever regain control over my own body again.

As the reality of my situation sank in, a wave of panic washed over me, making it difficult to breathe. I lay there, helpless and overwhelmed, trying to process the gravity of my newfound limitations. At that moment, every minute felt like an eternity, and I grappled with the fear of an unknown future. Despite the darkness surrounding me, a flicker of hope emerged, urging me to hold onto the possibility of recovery.

My colleagues called an ambulance and transported me to the KPJ Ipoh Specialist Hospital. The paramedics were very careful to keep my neck immobilized with a cervical collar. Once at the hospital, doctors began a series of tests to assess the full extent of my injuries. I could feel the weight of uncertainty pressing down on me as I faced the unknown road to recovery. As the tests continued, I found myself grappling with fears of what my future might hold. The beeping machines reminded me of life's fragility and encouraged me to face the challenges ahead.

An emergency MRI of the brain and neck was done at the hospital before being taken to the ICU. By now, it was already past midnight. The MRI showed a prolapse disc at C4 causing compression to the spinal cord. The diagnosis sent a chill through me, as the reality of my situation began to sink in. I knew this would require a long road to recovery. With determination, I reminded myself that I would face each challenge head-on, regardless of the obstacles ahead. I clung to hope, knowing that every day was a step toward healing and reclaiming my life.

The low hum of the fluorescent lights overhead seemed to add to the atmosphere of tension and anxiety. I closed my eyes for a moment, trying to gather the strength to confront whatever lay ahead. As I opened my eyes, the weight of uncertainty pressed heavily on my chest, but I felt a flicker of courage igniting within me. I took a deep breath, ready to embrace the journey and all its unpredictability.

SPINAL SURGERY

On the next day, a CT scan was done to provide a more detailed evaluation of the prolapsed intervertebral disc. Although the spinal shock had subsided somewhat, I remained tetraplegic. The spinal surgeon emphasized the importance of immediate surgery to relieve pressure on my spinal cord caused by a prolapsed intervertebral disc. His words filled me with a mix of dread and hope, as I realized this procedure might be my way to recovery. With each passing moment, I fortified my resolve, committed to battling for the future I envisioned. With every passing moment, I steeled myself for the outcome,

The surgeon cautioned me that the operation was delicate and carries a risk of permanent spastic tetraplegia if complications occur. On December 27, 2019, in the evening, I went into the operating theater for a major operation. The anesthetist gave me pure oxygen and general anesthesia to put me to sleep. As the anesthesia took effect, I felt a wave of calm wash over me, momentarily pushing my fears aside. I surrendered to the darkness, trusting the team of experts who surrounded me, hoping they could bring me back to the life I had yearned for.

REHABILITATION

I woke up to doctors urging me to wake up after my surgery. The sounds around me felt distant, like echoes in a tunnel, as I slowly began to regain consciousness. Blinking in the bright light, I felt relief and confused about the surgery and my upcoming rehabilitation journey. The memories of the operation were hazy, but I could sense the importance of this next chapter. I decided to face the challenges ahead because they were essential for regaining my strength and independence.

The clock on the wall showed 11 p.m, and I was transported back to the ICU. I could hear the soft hum of machines and the occasional shuffle of nurses outside my room. Each passing moment reminded me of the fragility of life, fueling my determination to recover fully and embrace the future.

After eight days of hospitalization, my condition had improved enough for me to be discharged in a wheelchair. Following six additional weeks of outpatient physiotherapy and rehabilitation, my condition improved further. During this time, the COVID-19 pandemic caused a nationwide lockdown. It took me two more months to be able to walk with a walking stick, unassisted. As my strength gradually returned, I felt a renewed sense of hope with every step I took. Every small victory made me appreciate my progress even more. I began to focus on setting new goals, determined to regain the life I once had. I started by incorporating daily exercises into my routine, pushing myself to increase my stamina and mobility. With each passing day, I became more confident in my abilities, excited to embrace the future ahead. I realized that each challenge I overcame only fueled my determination further. This newfound resilience motivated me to pursue activities I had neglected, igniting a passion to enjoy every moment.

THANK GOD WITH A GRATEFUL HEART

I am immensely thankful to God for preserving my life after experiencing spinal shock and spastic tetraplegia. I wholeheartedly credit my successful spinal surgery and rehabilitation to His miraculous intervention. Each day, I seek to embrace life fully, recognizing the beauty in the little things I once took for granted. I strive to cherish each sunrise and the laughter shared with loved ones, understanding that every moment is a gift. This deep appreciation has transformed my outlook, allowing me to find joy in even the simplest of experiences. As I navigate this new chapter, I am reminded of the strength within me and the unwavering support of my family and friends. It's a journey of rediscovery, where faith and gratitude guide me toward hope and resilience.

I'm very grateful to my cardiologist colleagues for sending an ambulance and helping protect my neck during the transfer. I am thankful for the ongoing support from my wife, children, relatives, friends, colleagues, pastors, church members, schoolmates, and university classmates. I especially want to thank those who prayed, encouraged, supported, cared, visited, and even prepared meals for me. Their support and encouragement were greatly appreciated. As I reflect on this experience, I realize how essential community is during difficult times. It strengthens my resolve to pay it forward and offer the same love and kindness to others in need. I believe that by sharing our experiences and support, we can create a chain of kindness that uplifts everyone involved. This sense of unity fosters hope and resilience, reminding us that we are never truly alone in our struggles.

I want to thank all the medical professionals at KPJ Ipoh Specialist Hospital who took care of me during my hospital stay. Their dedication and compassion made a significant difference in my recovery journey. I appreciate their dedication to helping others and will remember their kindness as I move forward. I am inspired to carry this gratitude into my everyday life, seeking opportunities to spread kindness in my own community. It is through these small acts that we can collectively create a more compassionate world. Every effort counts, and even the simplest gestures can have a profound impact on those around us. Let us strive to uplift one another and foster a spirit of generosity and support.

NOTHING SHORT OF A MIRACLE

A colleague who saw everything said I fell on my head and stayed still for a few minutes. After that, I suddenly opened my eyes and started talking. His fear was dispelled when my spontaneous recovery made its appearance! It was as if the universe had intervened, granting me a second chance at life. From that day forward, I vowed to cherish every moment and live each day with renewed purpose. I found beauty in the ordinary and began to appreciate the little things that had once gone unnoticed. Gratitude filled my heart, driving me to connect more deeply with the people around me.

One of my sons, an anesthetist practicing in New Zealand, remarked that injuries like mine frequently lead to lasting paralysis. His acknowledgment of my situation made me even more aware of how fortunate I truly was. It inspired me to share my story and support others facing similar challenges, showing that hope can flourish even in tough situations. As I shared my journey, I discovered a community of resilient individuals who were also facing their own challenges. Together, we found strength in our shared experiences, transforming our struggles into a powerful source of encouragement for one another.

I discovered the power of kindness, reaching out to strangers and friends alike, sharing smiles and words of encouragement. Each day became an opportunity to create lasting memories, transforming my outlook on life as I embraced the journey ahead. I believed that my recovery from this incident was truly a miracle from God. With each passing moment, I felt more empowered and grateful for the lessons learned along the way. As I reflected on my journey, I realized that every setback had only fueled my determination to rise stronger. This new perspective shaped my path and inspired others to face their challenges with resilience.

LIVING IN GOD'S MERCY AND GRACE

An outpouring of prayers via WhatsApp messenger sustained me during this trying time. My wife and sister provided constant support around the clock. Meanwhile, my in-laws took me on outings outside of Ipoh during Chinese New Year of 2020 to boost my morale. These moments of togetherness reminded me of the importance of family and community in overcoming adversity. Their love and encouragement helped restore my hope and instilled a sense of gratitude in my heart.

I realized how important it is to rely on our loved ones during tough times. The compassion and kindness shown to me fostered a deeper appreciation for the blessings in my life. As we shared laughter and stories, I felt a renewed sense of strength emerging from within. These outings lifted my spirits and strengthened my family bonds, reminding me we're never alone in our struggles.

I thank God for preserving my life and enabling me to continue serving Him. His incredible love, compassion, mercy, and grace affected my life like never before. It was an overwhelming demonstration of His amazing love, mercy, and grace. Without His watchfulness and astounding grace, I would not have been able to recover from being bedridden to full mobility. I hope this testimony motivates others just as it did for me.

RETIREMENT

After 48 years of practicing medicine, I embraced retirement on my 68th birthday in 2020. Every day, I find an opportunity to reflect on the blessings I have received and to share His goodness with those around me. I hope my journey inspires others to seek His presence and find the power of faith. Deciding to leave my jobs at Perak Community Specialist Hospital and KPJ Ipoh Specialist Hospital was important. As a result, my beloved stethoscope is now part of a museum exhibit. I have officially ended my medical practice completely. This marks a new chapter in my life, one that I approach with both excitement and trepidation. I look forward to exploring opportunities that allow me to spread hope and healing in different ways.

After retiring, I committed myself to serving God at St. Andrews Presbyterian Church in Pengkalan, Ipoh, as a preacher, Bible teacher, and lay leader. Moreover, I embraced authorship, publishing, blogging, and podcasting—activities that were once just distant dreams. Retirement granted me the opportunity to engage in these passions that I had long thought were beyond my grasp. As I immerse myself in these endeavors, I find a renewed sense of purpose guiding me each day. This journey boosts my spiritual growth and helps me connect deeply with others, sharing stories and wisdom. Through this shared experience, I've formed meaningful relationships with members of the congregation and the broader community. Every interaction strengthens my faith and connection with others, guiding me as I grow in service and understanding.

I want to thank God for all the blessings He has given my family and me over the years. Each day, I strive to recognize and appreciate the small miracles that surround us. My gratitude inspires me to help others, spreading kindness and compassion. I want to show the love I've received through acts of service and inspire others to enjoy giving. Together, we can build a stronger, more supportive community where everyone feels valued and uplifted. By sharing our resources and time, we create a ripple effect of positivity that can transform lives. Let's work hand in hand to foster an environment of hope and encouragement for all. We uplift others and enhance our own lives with a deeper sense of purpose. As we unite in our efforts, we can cultivate a brighter future filled with connection and empathy.

From Stethoscope to Wisdom

From stethoscope to wisdom's light,

Through endless days and sleepless nights,
A healer's hands, a heart so true,
In every pulse, a life anew.

With every breath, a tale unfolds,
In whispered pain, in stories told.
The stethoscope, an ear to find
The beat of hope within the mind.

Yet more than charts or signs revealed,
It's in the soul that wounds are healed.
Through joy and tears, the years have shown,
The greatest wisdom's humbly grown.

For in the space where science ends,
Compassion blooms, and hearts mend.
From stethoscope to wisdom's grace,
A doctor finds his sacred place.

drandrewcskoh.com/poems

Chapter 9
Rediscovering Purpose in Retirement

EXCERPT

Retirement is not the end of life. It is a new beginning. A retired cardiologist reflects on transitioning from a medical career to a life of rediscovery. Learn how retirement can open doors to new passions, deeper faith, and continued engagement in your field. Embrace this new chapter with purpose and joy.

NEW CHAPTER

Retirement signifies a significant transformation in one's life. I felt uncertain about retiring after many years in cardiology. Leaving patient care, hospital meetings, ward rounds, and medical conferences was both freeing and intimidating. After five years in retirement, I can confidently say that life is full of exciting opportunities. You will find them if you are open to them! Exploring new hobbies, volunteering, and spending time with family have brought me immense joy and fulfillment.

Embracing this new chapter has allowed me to rediscover passions that had been overshadowed by my demanding career. My new pursuits have really enriched my life and given me a fresh perspective on what makes me happy. I have learned to value the small things. I now appreciate quiet mornings with a cup of coffee. These are things that I used to take for granted. Each day feels like a gift, opening doors to experiences I never thought I'd have the time for.

I seek adventure in everyday activities, like walking in the park or trying new recipes at home. This newfound appreciation for life has sparked a sense of gratitude that permeates my everyday experiences. As I embrace this mindset, I find myself more connected to the world around me and the people in it. It's as if each moment becomes a treasure, reminding me to savor the beauty of the ordinary.

With every small interaction, I discover the joy in shared laughter and the warmth of genuine conversation. This shift in perspective has transformed my life into a vibrant tapestry of moments worth cherishing. I have learned to celebrate the little victories and find meaning in the simplest of tasks. Each day unfolds with the promise of new experiences, inviting me to explore and engage more deeply with my surroundings.

NEWFOUND FREEDOM

For a cardiologist, retirement is not just quitting a job. It is stepping away from a life filled with urgency, responsibility, and learning for over 30 years. My day-to-day life consisted of diagnosing and managing heart conditions. I performed procedures and gave hope to my patients during times of vulnerability.

I am now involved in a space that promotes thinking and creativity. This environment allows me to focus on my well-being. I can now pursue interests I had ignored before. This newfound freedom, I believe, is a gift that encourages personal growth and deeper connections with those I hold dear. Each day is an opportunity to cultivate not just my hobbies, but also to nurture relationships that enrich my soul. As I engage with others who share similar passions,

I find inspiration in their stories and experiences. These interactions fuel my wish to explore even more facets of life, creating a tapestry of shared knowledge and joy. Through these connections, I am reminded of the beauty of community and the strength we draw from one another. Together, we embark on journeys that expand our horizons and deepen our understanding of the world around us.

In this ever-changing landscape of life, every meeting holds the potential to teach us something new. I cherish the moments when laughter and wisdom intertwine, leaving lasting impressions that guide my path ahead. I am becoming more open to embracing change and unexpected life turns. Each lesson learned becomes a stepping stone, shaping my perspective and enriching my journey.

REDISCOVERING PURPOSE

One of the greatest joys of retirement has been rediscovering my true identity beyond professional practice. I have engaged in activities that make me truly happy. These activities have allowed me to discover talents I didn't fully develop while working. This journey of self-discovery has renewed my enthusiasm and helped me connect with the world more meaningfully.

With each new venture, I've found myself embracing new challenges that push my boundaries and broaden my perspective. My sense of adventure drives me to keep learning and growing, making my days purposeful and exciting. I cherish the moments that come from stepping outside my comfort zone, as they often lead to unexpected rewards.

Every experience teaches me something valuable, adding depth to my understanding of myself and the world around me. As I continue to explore new horizons, I am reminded that growth often stems from the willingness to take risks. These lessons shape my identity and inspire me to share my journey, encouraging others to explore their own paths.

By sharing my experiences, I hope to ignite a spark in others, motivating them to embrace their unique adventures. Ultimately, the richness of life lies in our ability to connect, learn, and grow together through our diverse journeys. Through these connections, we cultivate empathy and a deeper appreciation for the stories that weave us together. In this shared tapestry of life, each thread represents the unique experiences and perspectives that enhance our collective understanding.

MAINTAINING CONNECTIONS

Even though I no longer practice medicine in its traditional sense, my passion for cardiology still burns bright. As I think about these experiences, I realize that each lesson shapes my path ahead. This ongoing evolution not only enriches my life but also fosters deeper connections with those I meet along the way.

I stay updated by attending conferences whenever I can and keep contact with former colleagues. Through these connections, I gain insights into the latest advancements and trends in the field. This ongoing engagement allows me to merge my medical knowledge with my newfound purpose in writing and sharing wisdom.

By articulating my experiences, I not only help others navigate their challenges but also continue to learn about myself. Every story I share adds to my journey, creating a rich narrative that inspires both me and those around me. I enjoy turning complex medical ideas into relatable stories as I explore the connection between medicine and storytelling. As I think about these stories, I realize how interconnected our experiences are, forming a tapestry of resilience and hope.

This realization fuels my passion to empower others through my words, fostering a sense of community and understanding. These narratives not only educate but also inspire others to embark on their own journeys of discovery and growth. I try to connect the complex world of medicine with human experiences. I do this by incorporating personal stories and professional insights into my writing. Ultimately, my goal is to empower readers to understand and appreciate the profound impact of health on their lives.

EXPLORING NEW INTERESTS

One of the unexpected joys of retirement has been exploring interests I never had time for while practicing medicine. I have started writing my autobiography, books, and poems. These nourish my spirit and give me a sense of achievement. This experience shows that it is never too late to learn something new. You can express yourself, regardless of your age or life experience!

Each book and poem become a reflection of my journey. They capture the essence of faith and hope that sustains me. Embracing creativity not only enriches my life but also connects me with others who share similar passions and experiences. Through this shared connection, I find inspiration and strength to continue exploring new avenues of expression.

Ultimately, these creative pursuits remind me that life is a continuous journey of growth and discovery. As I navigate this journey, I embrace each challenge as an opportunity for learning and self-improvement. With every step ahead, I cultivate a deeper understanding of myself and the world around me. I create an environment for growth and collaboration by surrounding myself with like-minded people.

FAITH AND REFLECTION

Retirement has given me an opportunity to deepen my relationship with God. This understanding fuels my wish to innovate and push boundaries, encouraging me to take risks in my creative endeavors. This process fuels my wish to innovate and create, pushing me to step outside my comfort zone. Each new experience adds another layer to my personal narrative, shaping the way I perceive the beauty in everyday moments.

This process transforms obstacles into building blocks, allowing me to weave a richer tapestry of experiences. Each moment spent in creative exploration deepens my appreciation for the beauty and complexity of life itself. This ongoing process shapes my identity and fuels my wish to innovate and create. This helps me grow as a person and adds to our collective human experience.

Now that I am retired and have more time for reflection, I can better understand how my faith influences my life. Blogging, writing, and podcasting have helped me share my faith journey with others to grow spiritually. Retirement has felt like a spiritual rebirth, allowing me to think about how grace has guided my life. Every day offers an opportunity to inspire others and be inspired. It is a time to celebrate the colorful tapestry of life created by faith and creativity.

I dedicate more time to prayer, meditation, contemplation, reflection, and studying the Bible. This deeper engagement with my spiritual practices has enriched my understanding and connection to God. Contemplation and reflection strengthen my faith. As I immerse myself in these practices, I find a renewed sense of purpose and clarity in my life's direction. Every lesson learned strengthens my connection with God and motivates me to spread this positivism to others.

TAKEAWAYS

Retiring does not signal an end; rather it marks a new chapter waiting to be written. Retirement has allowed me to rediscover, contemplate, and renew myself. While I'm no longer practicing medicine, I stay connected to cardiology through pursuits that show my passion. I find fulfillment in sharing my knowledge and experience. This new phase in life has unveiled endless possibilities for growth and connection that I never anticipated.

Retirement is the perfect opportunity to unwind, embrace relaxation, and savor the rewards of my hard work. I've taken up various hobbies that challenge my creativity and intellect, like writing. Each day, I explore the world through new lenses, enhancing my life in surprising and profound ways.

Are you getting ready to retire? Embrace it as an opportunity to explore, create, and grow rather than fearing it. Retirement can offer fulfillment and joy by allowing you to redefine success and pursue new opportunities.

Chapter 10
A Friendship Story of Onions and Sugar Canes

INTRODUCTION

In today's fast-paced world, there's an unparalleled comfort in revisiting the cherished memories of our school days. These formative experiences mold us in profound ways that often only become clear much later in life. Join me as I think about my time at Methodist English Primary School in Tanjong Malim, Malaysia.

This story is not just about academics. It includes joyful traditions, surprising superstitions, and an amazing reunion after almost fifty years. As I delve into those influential years, I'm flooded with memories of laughter and camaraderie. Every moment offers valuable lessons, both in and out of the classroom, that have shaped who I am today.

PRIMARY SCHOOL BEGINNINGS

It all started in 1959, when I embarked on my educational journey at Methodist English Primary School. While I may not remember every detail from those early years, one memory stands out vividly. It is my first day of school.

In a charmingly superstitious gesture, my parents secretly placed onions and sugar canes in my school bag. Why, you ask? Well, according to Cantonese tradition, onions symbolizes intelligence, and they hoped it would boost my intelligence. Similarly, sugar cane represented sweetness, and they believed it would make me into a sweet person.

When a classmate rummaged through my bag and found strange items, everyone laughed, and I felt embarrassed. What I did not expect was that this classmate would soon evolve into my closest friend. We connected over our shared sense of humour and passion for all things quirky.

From that moment on, we proudly embraced our individuality and celebrated the delightful oddities that united us. Our adventures were filled with spontaneous outings and inside jokes that only we understood. It was truly refreshing to find someone who cherished the eccentricities of life as much as I did.

A REMARKABLE FRIENDSHIP

The classmate who discovered the unusual items in my bag became my closest friend during primary school. We spent endless time exploring the school library, lost in books and discovering new worlds through literature. Our shared love for music led us to tune in to the radio for the latest pop songs.

We listened to artists of the 1960s, like Cliff Richard, Herman's Hermits, Bee Gees, Beatles, Seekers, and so on. Those melodies became the soundtrack of our friendship, creating memories that would last a lifetime. Singing our favorite songs, we dreamed of future adventures beyond school.

My friend had a unique style, emulating Elvis Presley with his signature high hairstyle. But that wasn't all. He also had a soft spot for Mary Poppins and even adopted the nickname, *Poppy Leong*. Our days were filled with spinning tops, catapults, and marbles.

We also enjoyed the thrill of capturing fighting fish from nearby rivers and spiders from towering trees. We pedaled our classic bicycles to the charming towns nearby. These adventures kept our spirits high and friendship strong, as we explored the world around us with a childlike wonder.

Every day felt like a new chapter, filled with laughter and the music that united us. We soared kites, played games, and embraced our roles as enthusiastic members of the Boy Scouts. Our school days were a vibrant tapestry of thrilling adventures and collective experiences. Each moment was a precious memory in the making, with every escapade deepening our connection.

As we navigated through childhood, those carefree days shaped who we would become, forever etched in our hearts. We would gather around campfires, sharing stories that sparked our imagination and forged lasting friendships. In those moments, surrounded by the warmth of community, we discovered the true essence of connection and belonging.

A BITTERSWEET FAREWELL

Like all beautiful things, my treasured friendship took an unexpected turn. One day, my closest friend abruptly left school without even saying goodbye. I was left in a state of confusion and heartache. He had casually mentioned the chance of moving to another town with his family. Still, he provided no forwarding location or any means of staying in touch.

Days turned into weeks, and the silence only deepened my sense of loss. I often think about our good times and wonder if we will reconnect someday. Yet, as time passes, I find solace in the memories we created together. Every joyful moment reminds me that even if we go our separate ways, those experiences will always be special.

They will always hold a special place in my heart. Those experiences will always be special to me. For years, I pondered over the mysterious end of our friendship. It felt like an unfinished chapter, a narrative longing for closure. Even when I thought I had moved on, memories of our laughter and shared adventures came back to me.

They reminded me of our strong connection. I often imagined what life would have been like if we had managed to reconnect. The unanswered questions loomed over me like shadows, persistent and haunting. As time passed, I realized that some mysteries are meant to stay unsolved, etched into the fabric of my memories.

Yet, the longing for that lost connection still tugged at my heart, refusing to fade away completely. Even after all this time, I still hoped to see him again and understand why he left so suddenly. I couldn't shake the feeling that there was more to our story than what had been written.

Perhaps one day, we will find the opportunity to rewrite the ending together. Until then, I carry these memories like fragile keepsakes, longing for the day when they can be shared once more. Each heartbeat reminds me of the moments that still linger in the corners of my heart.

I often find myself lost in thought, wondering what could have been if life had played out differently. Yet, in those quiet moments, I also remind myself that every ending holds the promise of a new beginning.

REUNION AFTER 48 YEARS

In 2015, something extraordinary took place. After an astonishing 48 years apart, I was reunited with my long-lost friend, thanks to the wonders of modern technology. Social media platforms like Facebook, Google, WhatsApp messenger, and email were instrumental in facilitating our re-connection. The moment I received his message was surreal. It felt like a bridge across time had just been built. It brought back memories, stories, and laughter, reigniting the bond that had never truly faded.

To my surprise, he was then residing in Jakarta, Indonesia. I made not just one, but two trips to Jakarta exclusively to reconnect with my dear friend. The years had made him forget about onions, sugar cane, and his signature Elvis Presley hairstyle. He had even lost touch with his cherished nickname, *Poppy Leong*.

As we reminisced, memories started to return, and Poppy's laughter filled the bustling city streets. Each conversation felt like reclaiming a part of ourselves we thought was lost forever. Together, we wandered through vibrant markets, sampling street food and sharing stories, breathing life back into our friendship. In those sunny moments, it felt like time rewound, helping us reconnect with the bond of our youth.

Each moment felt like a cherished flashback, underscoring the belief that true connections withstand the test of time and distance. As we walked through the busy markets, the smell of street food brought back memories of our adventures together. It was a reminder that while some things fade, the joy of companionship blooms anew with every reunion.

A SAD FAREWELL

It is with a heavy heart that I share the loss of my best friend. He passed away peacefully in Jakarta in 2020 after battling lymphoma. He leaves behind his beloved wife, and I take solace in knowing that we will reunite in the next life. Rest in peace, my dear friend.

The memories we created together will forever be etched in my heart, guiding me through the moments of sorrow. I will cherish each laugh, every adventure, and the unbreakable bond we shared. The world feels a little dimmer without him.

I hold onto the laughter we shared. The bond we had can never be broken. In every gathering, I find pieces of him in our shared stories and the memories that linger in the air. Each smile and every tear remind me that love transcends time and distance, keeping his spirit alive within me.

I find comfort in the stories we share, and the love felt by those who knew him. As I navigate this journey of grief, I find solace. I think about how he will always be a part of me. He shapes who I am. Though the road ahead be uncertain, the warmth of our memories will guide me through the darkness.

His spirit lingers in my heart, a gentle reminder of the moments that once brought me joy. His legacy inspires me to value our connections and celebrate life fully, even though he is gone. I strive to honour his memory by fostering those relationships and cherishing every moment with my loved ones.

Each day I cherished the laughter and love we shared, proving he will never be forgotten. In every smile, every shared memory, I can feel his presence guiding me onward. I hold onto the belief that love transcends time, keeping us connected despite the distance imposed by loss.

During life's challenges, I find comfort knowing he silently supports me from a distance. This unwavering bond reminds me to live passionately and to embrace each day with gratitude and joy.

Chapter 11
A Journey Back to the House We Called Home

EXCERPT

The narrative reflects on a 60-year journey back to a cherished home, where seven individuals created lifelong memories. The 2018 reunion captures nostalgia as they recreate a significant photograph from 1958. The house symbolizes their shared history. It emphasizes the importance of family bonds, cherished moments, and the enduring connections formed over time.

GROWING UP IN OUR BELOVED HOME

In 1958, seven of us found a home in this house, brimming with youth and bursting with hopes and dreams. We shared laughter and crafted memories that would forever influence our lives. This house was the epicenter of everything. It was a sanctuary of comfort, love, and family.

As seasons changed, the walls witnessed our triumphs and trials, each room echoing the stories of our growth. It became a haven where the warmth of friendship flourished, and the bonds of family strengthened. Every corner held a piece of our history, each photograph a reminder of moments that shaped us. No matter where life takes us, the essence of this home will always stay in our hearts.

SEIZING THE MOMENT: THE ICONIC PHOTO

In 1958, we made the decision to immortalize a significant moment with a photograph. Standing side by side, we were blissfully unaware of the paths that lay ahead for us. At that moment, it was just a simple picture. Yet, it would evolve into a treasured symbol of a pivotal chapter in our lives. We would hold this chapter dear for all time.

Years later, that photo would serve as a reminder of our shared laughter and the dream we once held close. As we gazed upon it, we realized how far we had come and how those moments had shaped our identities. Each look at that treasured image brings back memories, reminding us of our youthful innocence. It showed how strong our bond is. It reminded us that, despite life's changes, that moment will always be part of us.

A JOURNEY BACK: REFLECTING ON 50 YEARS SINCE 1958

Sixty years later, in 2018, life has led us down various paths filled with adventures, personal trials, and transformations. Despite the passage of time, we all found our way back to the house where it all began. The miles that separated us did not matter. As we stepped inside, a wave of nostalgia swept over us, instantly transporting us back to our youthful days. The familiar creaks of the floorboards echoed memories of laughter and dreams shared among friends.

It felt like time had folded in on itself, wrapping us in nostalgia as we rediscovered our enduring bonds. Every corner of the house held a story, each room a chapter of our collective history. We reminisced about the moments that shaped us, feeling grateful for the opportunity to reconnect and celebrate our journey.

REVIVING A TIMLESS MEMORY: THE SECOND PHOTO

We stood once again in the exact positions captured in the original 1958 photo, recreating that cherished moment. While the house had weathered the years, as had we, our bond remained unwavering. The 2018 photo was more than just a recreation; it celebrated the many years of memories that brought us together. As we posed for the photo, our laughter filled the air, each smile reflecting our journey together.

We realized that, although time changed our looks, it strengthened our love and memories. At that moment, we were surrounded by familiarity and nostalgia. We felt like we had traveled back in time. We reconnected with our younger selves. Comparing the past and the present highlights our progress while showing how connected our lives still are.

THE IMPACT OF CHERISHED MEMORIES

As we reflected on the years gone by, we grasped the profound significance of returning to this house. It was more than just a building; it represented our history, our stories, and who we had become. The house and its cherished memories serve as a timeless bond, connecting us regardless of where life may take us.

Every corner whispered tales of laughter and tears, moments that shaped us into the people we are today. The roots of our family would always bring us back home, no matter how far we may wander. In the warmth of its familiar embrace, we found solace and strength, reigniting the love that fueled our journey. We celebrated our shared past, highlighting the lasting impact of memory on our lives.

SHARE YOUR UNIQUE STORY

Is there a cherished place or memory that links you to your past? Take a moment to think about the locations and individuals who have influenced your journey. It could be a childhood park where friendships formed and dreams began, filled with summer warmth and joyful laughter. Reflecting on these moments can profoundly influenced your values and aspirations.

Whether it's a photograph, a visit, or a heartfelt conversation, reconnect with those pivotal moments. If you have had similar experiences, I invite you to share your story! These memories remind you on how lives are connected and how the past influences the present. Embracing these influences can empower you to forge ahead with renewed purpose and clarity.

Celebrate the deep significance of family and the journey of time spent together. By crafting new memories that pay tribute to your history, you pave the way for a more radiant future. Every relationship you cultivate enhances your life and fortifies the ties that bind.

Two Photos

Two photos on the wall,
Captured moments, time's soft call.
One, a face from years long past,
Frozen smiles that couldn't last.

The other, newer yet just as dear,
A younger face, without the years.
Side by side, both worlds collide,
In the space where memories reside.

One tells stories, weathered, wise,
Of love, of loss, of distant skies.
The other whispers dreams untold,
The future bright, the path yet bold.

Two photos, yet a single tale,
Of life's journey, long and frail.
Moments stitched through joy and pain,
Of hearts entwined, again, again.

www.drandrewcskoh.com/poems

The Lord is My Shepherd

The Lord is my Shepherd, I shall not fear,He guides my steps, His voice I hear.In pastures green, He leads me still,Beside the waters, calm and chill.
He restores my soul when I'm worn thin,His love surrounds, His peace within.
Though shadows dark may block my way,With Him, I know I will not stray.
His rod and staff, they comfort me,In His embrace, I am set free.My cup overflows with blessings untold,His mercy follows, His grace I hold.
Through every valley, high and low,He walks beside me, this I know.In Him, my trust, my hope, my song,The Shepherd' s love will lead me strong.

www.drandrewcxskoh.com/poems

Chapter 12
From Fall to Recovery

EXCERPT

After suffering a painful fall in my garden, I embarked on a journey of healing and gratitude. From surgery to rehabilitation, each step taught me resilience. It deepened my faith in God. It strengthened my connection to the people who supported me. This is a reflection on transformation, hope, and the power of gratitude.

FALL

On July 27, 2024, I fell in my garden and injured my left leg. The pain made even the slightest movement excruciating, and I could not get up independently. My son kindly and skilfully assisted me into the car, navigating the process with utmost care. As we drove to the hospital, my mind raced with concerns, dreading what the doctors might reveal about my condition.

I was astonished by the depth of gratitude I felt for the unwavering support of my loved ones. Their presence transformed a daunting experience into a more manageable one, providing me with comfort through their relentless encouragement. As we approached the hospital, I inhaled deeply, bracing myself for the journey ahead.

Upon arriving, the weight of reality hit me hard, but I clutched my son's hand tightly. Together, we entered through the doors, united by hope and a resolute determination to confront the challenges that lay ahead.

DIAGNOSIS

My left leg remained excruciatingly painful until we arrived at the accident and emergency department of a private hospital. A physician conducted a thorough examination of my left leg and suspected a fracture. An X-ray later confirmed the diagnosis. My left femur was fractured at the neck. Given the severity of the injury, an orthopaedic surgeon was summoned promptly.

The orthopaedic surgeon reviewed my X-ray results and recommended an emergency left hip joint replacement (hemiarthroplasty). He thoroughly explained the surgery, detailing each step and what I could expect during the recovery process. As I prepared for the surgery, I felt nervous. Yet, I was determined. I knew this was my only chance to regain my mobility.

SURGERY

As I was wheeled into the operating room, I focused on the possibility of walking pain-free again. The surrounding team buzzed with efficiency, reassuring me that I was in capable hands. The anaesthesiologist put a mask on my face, and I took a deep breath, feeling my worries fade away. Darkness began to envelop me. I held on to the hope that this surgery would mark the beginning of a new chapter in my life.

Upon awakening, I realized the surgery was finished, and I was being transported back to the ward. I gradually became aware of my surroundings, hearing the soft beeping of monitors and seeing my nurse nearby. A wave of relief washed over me.

I attempted to move my legs. I felt the first hints of new freedom. The dull ache reminded me that recovery was just beginning, but it also reaffirmed my determination to heal. Surrounded by the antiseptic smell and quiet buzz of the hospital, I realized I was starting to reclaim my life.

The surgery was very successful. I am happy to say that the severe pain I used to feel has greatly reduced. It is a remarkable transformation from the unbearable existence I faced before the operation. At last, I can envision the life I have always dreamed of and liberated from relentless discomfort. With each passing moment, I am filled with renewed optimism and deep gratitude for the journey that lies ahead.

As my recovery progressed, I came to appreciate the countless things I had formerly taken for granted. The simple pleasures of daily life are now more vivid and significant than ever before. Each moment feels like a precious treasure. I am eager to embark on this new chapter with an optimistic mindset.

REHABILITATION

After several days in the ward, I transitioned to outpatient care. I committed myself to weekly rehabilitation sessions, each one presenting a fresh challenge. With each step I took, I felt increasingly stronger and more resolute. Surrounded by a supportive community, my optimism for my recovery journey blossomed.

I began by establishing small, achievable goals for myself. The support from my peers and the guidance from my therapists ignited my motivation to persevere. As the weeks passed, I saw remarkable progress in both my physical strength and mental resilience.

This newfound confidence became a powerful source of encouragement for me. With each day that passed, I welcomed the promise of a brighter future. I discovered that my journey was not just about recovery, but also about uncovering my true potential and identity.

As I reflected on my experiences, I recognized that every challenge I encountered was a chance for growth. I learned to embrace uncertainty and view it as an opportunity rather than a setback. This shift in perspective allowed me to navigate life's obstacles with a sense of purpose and determination.

I found strength in vulnerability, understanding that sharing my struggles could inspire others on a similar path. Every step ahead felt like a victory, showing me that resilience and hope can thrive even in tough times.

Embracing this mindset transformed my approach to adversity and deepened my connections with others. Each person's story became a source of inspiration, reminding me that we are never truly alone in our journeys.

THANK GOD WITH A GRATEFUL HEART

I am profoundly grateful to God for His boundless mercy and unwavering grace throughout my challenging journey. From the fall to the surgery, rehabilitation, and recovery, His steadfast protection has been a source of strength. With a humble heart, I express my deepest appreciation to Him for the incredible blessings He has granted me.

This journey has profoundly deepened my reliance on God's strength. Apostle Paul reminds me that His grace is more than enough for me. My weaknesses become my strengths through Him. In my moments of weakness, His power shines bright. I see life's challenges as opportunities for spiritual growth, transforming every trial into a vital stepping stone on my journey.

These experiences have deepened my sense of purpose and connection to Him. This journey reassures me that I am never alone; His presence guides me at every turn. During the darkest moments, His light shines the brightest, illuminating the path before me.

I am thankful for the strength I get from this relationship, knowing that every struggle is full of His grace. God surely has a higher purpose behind every event that unfolds. In the Kingdom of God, nothing happens by chance. Every experience teaches me important lessons. These lessons strengthen my character and faith.

As I navigate this journey, I embrace each moment with unwavering hope and trust in His divine plan. With every challenge I face, I draw closer to Him and rely more on His Strength. Although this journey may be challenging, it is transforming me into the person He intended me to become.

FOREVER GRATEFUL

I am incredibly grateful to the orthopaedic surgeon, anaesthetist, and the entire medical team for their exceptional care and support. Their unmatched knowledge, skill, and unwavering commitment have been crucial in navigating me through this challenging journey. I will forever treasure their support and compassion, which have been vital to my recovery. This experience has deepened my faith and heightened my appreciation for those who dedicate their lives to healing others.

I am deeply appreciative of the exceptional care provided by the hospital staff, nursing team, and paramedical personnel. Their unwavering commitment to excellence and tireless dedication significantly affected my recovery. In moments when I needed peace and comfort, they were there for me. Their kindness and professionalism fostered an atmosphere where I felt secure and supported. I will forever cherish the compassion they showed during my time of need.

I am profoundly grateful to everyone who has contributed to my healing journey. Their kindness and support have not only transformed my life but have also positively affected countless others. Inspired by their example, I want to pay it back and show compassion to others facing similar challenges. I aim to honour their legacy by actively supporting and showing empathy to those in need.

Every small act of kindness has the power to create a ripple effect, transforming the world for the better. By embracing the spirit of generosity, I aspire to inspire others to follow suit. Together, we can nurture a community where kindness thrives, and empathy prevails.

In doing so, we create an environment where everyone feels valued and supported. This collective effort can lead to remarkable changes, fostering hope and resilience in those who need it most.

I firmly believe that through collective efforts, we can fundamentally transform lives and cultivate an atmosphere of unwavering support. This dedication to giving back not only elevates the lives of others but also profoundly enriches our own.

Together, we are forging a hopeful future grounded in our shared humanity. By consistently engaging in acts of kindness, we are laying the foundation for a brighter tomorrow. Every small gesture matters, highlighting the immense power we have when we unite.

From Garden to Surgery

It began in the garden, so peaceful, so
bright,The sun kissed the blooms in the
warm morning light.But one sudden
slip, and the earth met my fall,In a
moment, my world grew painfully small.

The pain in my leg was sharp and
severe,My son lifted me up, his strength
held me near.With each breath, the ache
only grew,To the hospital's doors, our
path quickly flew.

An X-ray revealed what my body had
known,A fracture, a break deep in the
bone.The surgeon arrived, calm and
precise,A new hip awaited, no time to
think twice.

From garden to surgery, a whirlwind of
care,
Prayers in my heart, hope in the air.The
knife was sharp, the hands were skilled,
And soon, my pain was finally stilled.

Two days later, I stood once more,With
a walker to help, my feet found the
floor.A week had passed, and I was free,
Grateful for life and new mobility.

From garden to surgery, a chapter now
past,But strength and healing are
coming fast.In every step, I carry grace,A
newfound hope in every pace.

www.drandrewcskoh.com/poems

Postscript

My dear family, our children amuse us with their playful and silly behavior. It's like they have discovered the true meaning of being adorable. Cats and puppies prance around in adorable ways without even trying; yet their charm remains undeniable. Likewise, with our children, such moments become treasured memories forever remembered by grandparents; here we become entranced by their innocence and endearing childlike spirit.

God has given us wonderful children who bring joy to our lives with their playful and enthusiastic nature. I hope that you share this memoir with your little blessings just like I plan to do, for my love for them knows no boundaries!

May God shower His grace upon all of us and may His mercy prevail upon our lives.

With love comes devotion.

Grandma Wai Yin

February 2021

A doc's calling

Through endless halls and quiet
rooms,
He battles fears and silent dooms.
With every step, a life to save,
A weary heart, yet always brave.

In moments brief, he finds
reprieve,
In lives renewed, in pain they
leave.
A child's first breath, a mother's
tears,
A doc's reward through all the
years.

With stethoscope and tender care,
He faces loss, he learns to bear.
The weight of sorrow, joy's
embrace,
A human soul, in every face.

Though nights are long and rest is
rare,
He finds his strength in whispered
prayer.
For every life, a precious gift,
A doc's true calling, hearts to lift.

www.drandrewcskoh.com/poems

Epilogue

Finally, I want to add an epilogue to my memoir to cover any missed elements and conclude my life story. This memoir chronicles significant events from 1952 to 2024, detailing an extraordinary journey that spans 72 years. Nonetheless, it does not capture every experience from that period. In the book, I have written about the lessons, resilience, and gratitude that I gained from challenges and connections from the past.

I apologize for any errors or oversights that may have occurred because of my imperfect memory over time. Ultimately, the essence of this memoir lies in the moments that shaped me and the stories that created lasting memories. I hope readers find inspiration in my journey and our shared human experience. Through my reflections, I aim to illuminate the universal truths that bind us all together. Each chapter not only retells my life but also invites others to explore their own narratives and the power of storytelling.

Here is one story that I have left out in the book. I have warm memories of the European missionaries who came to my hometown in the 1960s to share the Gospel. They dedicated themselves to learning Chinese dialects and Mandarin to connect with the local community. They used portable blackboards and projectors, which made their teaching engaging and sparked my interest, especially during the film presentations. The excitement was clear as images on the screen took us to places we had only dreamed of. These experiences taught me how storytelling can connect cultures and inspire a love of learning.

Upon my retirement in 2020, the Covid-19 pandemic, which originated in Wuhan, China, quickly spread around the world, including Malaysia. In response, the government enforced nationwide lockdowns starting in March 2020, impacting every corner of the country. Subsequently, Malaysia implemented a vaccination program for the whole country. With rising vaccination rates, a sense of normalcy returned, and communities reconnected and supported one another. This resilience demonstrated the strength of the human spirit in overcoming challenges and highlighted the need for unity and understanding in tough times.

Since then, I dedicated much of my leisure time to writing books. By God's grace, I have written and published 36 books by 2024. This achievement fulfilled my lifelong dream and let me share my stories with a wider audience. I wanted to inspire others and positively impact the community through my writing. Each book became a vessel for the experiences and lessons I had gathered over the years. Seeing my words resonate with readers was a profound reminder of the power of storytelling.

This book is the culmination of countless hours dedicated to my craft at the computer. During this writing journey, I have surpassed my own expectations, developed new skills, gained valuable knowledge, made lasting friendships, and embraced new perspectives. The Holy Spirit has been my steadfast guide, providing unwavering support and wisdom every step of the way. Reflecting on this journey, I feel grateful for the inspiring moments that sparked my creativity.

To conclude, let me quote from Isaiah 40:26: *"Look to the heavens: Who created all these stars? Their Creator brings them out like an army, calling out each one by name." With His incredible power and incomparable strength, not one has gone amiss!*

This bible verse reminds us that each of our contributions, no matter how small, is significant in the grand tapestry of life. As you turn the pages of this book, I hope it serves not only as a testament to my journey but also as an inspiration for you to pursue your passions with faith and determination.

With warmest regards and deep appreciation.

A YEAR OF WRITING

2020, a year of writing,
unleashing the power of
healing.
A year of substantial
learning,
new writing skills for
acquiring,
new methodology
notwithstanding.
2020, a year of the mighty
pen,
writing to inform, teach, and
plan,
to convict, correct, train, and
 send,
reaching out to the mass.
2020, a year of blogging,
3000 followers and counting,
A year of unimaginable
suffering,
For everyone who is living.

andrewcskoh.com/poems

My Heart, Christ's Home

Lord, come dwell within my heart,
Make every corner Yours,
Cleanse each room with love and light,
Open all the doors.

The hallways where I hide my fears,
And closets filled with pride,
I offer now for You to clear—
No longer will I hide.

The dining room of selfish gain,
Where greed once took its place,
Now filled with hunger for Your name,
I feast upon Your grace.

In the study where my thoughts reside,
Renew my mind with truth,
The books and scrolls that glorify
Will echo You in proof.

The living room, once filled with shame,
Now hosts Your presence sweet.
You sit with me; I call Your name,
And rest beneath Your feet.

The bedroom, Lord, is wholly Yours,
A place where peace can bloom.
Guard me from storms of earthly wars,
And fill with holy room.

So walk, O Christ, within these walls,
With joy I welcome You.
My heart is Yours, for now and all,
Your home, forever true.

www.drandrewcskoh.com/poems

One Last Thing

Thank you for selecting my book. I genuinely hope it has offered you an enjoyable and stimulating experience. I would appreciate your feedback and would be grateful if you could write a review on the platform where you bought it or on a book review site. Your feedback will help others make choices and show me which parts of the book were effective or lacking. Your honest review will help me grow as a writer and motivate me to create more engaging stories in the future.

Thank you once again for taking the time to explore my book. I genuinely hope it proved to be a rewarding experience for you. Your support means everything to me, and I am truly grateful to each reader who joins me on this journey. Together, we can cultivate a vibrant community of readers and writers united by our love for storytelling.

Each review contributes to a vibrant dialogue that enriches our literary experience. I look forward to hearing your thoughts and insights as we continue to explore the depths of creativity together. Your feedback is invaluable, and it inspires me to keep pushing the boundaries of my writing. Let's keep the conversation going and delve deeper into the stories that connect us all.

Dr. Andrew C S Koh

Tyranny of the urgent

The clock, it ticks, a ruthless king,
Demanding every fleeting thing.
Tasks pile up, they suffocate,
With every breath, the weight is great.

A voice that whispers, Do it now,
You must, you will, I won't allow
A moment spared for peace or rest,
Urgency is what's best.

But in the rush, what do I lose?
The quiet moments I refuse,
The still, the small, the sacred call,
Drowned out by duties, one and all.

The urgent shouts, the need is loud,
A fleeting shadow, a passing cloud.
Yet in the stillness, wisdom waits,
A slower rhythm liberates.

I hear Him whisper in the storm,
Be still, My child, and be reformed.
The world may clamor for your time,
But peace is found in what's divine.

The tyranny of urgent things,
Can steal the joy that Heaven brings.
So I will choose to slow, to wait,
For in His presence, time is great.

No more the slave to rushing hours,
I'll trust in God's unhurried power.
For in the quiet, truth is heard,
And life is shaped by His own Word.

www.drandrewcskoh.com/poems

Top: Family
Bottom: School Reunion

Top: School Reunion
Bottom: My Parent's Grave

Top: Conference
Bottom: Family

Coronary Intervention

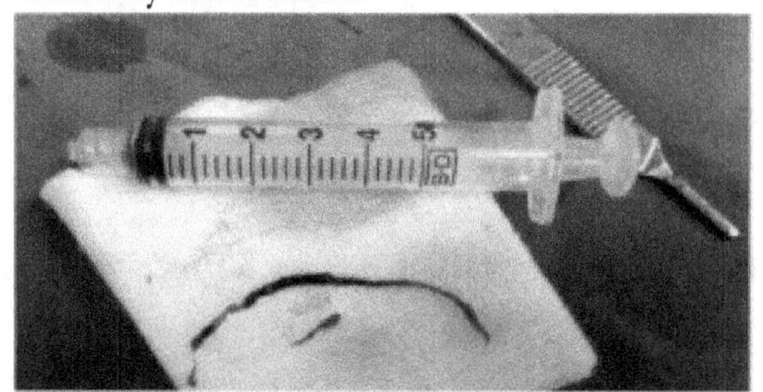

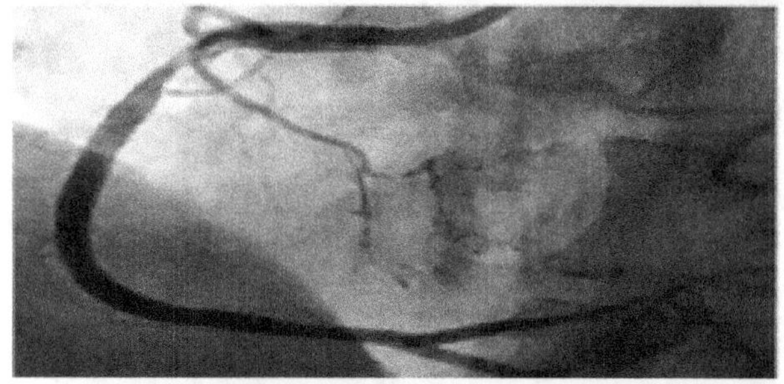

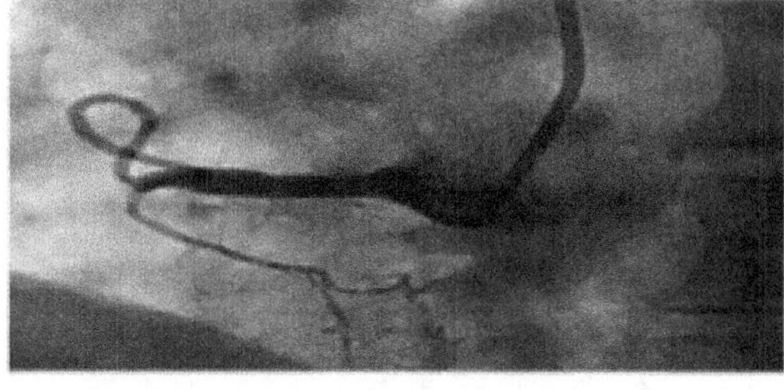

School Band

India

European Society of Cardiology Congress

Boy Scout

Me and my sons.

Boy Scouts

Book Haven- E-book Store

Scan QR code above for more information

Reflections of a Doctor

In quiet halls and sterile light,
I stood before both life and
night.
With trembling hands and
steadfast will,
I learned to heal, to mend, to
still.

I watched as hearts would
break and mend,
A thousand lives, their stories
blend.
In every beat, in every breath,
I walked the line between life
and death.

The stethoscope, my constant
guide,
Through whispered prayers, I
stood beside,
A soul in pain, a heart laid
bare,
I offered hope, a silent prayer.

drandrewcskoh.com/poems

Don't miss out!

Visit the website below and you can sign up to receive emails whenever Dr Andrew C S Koh publishes a new book. There's no charge and no obligation.

https://books2read.com/r/B-A-FMXV-SGCAF

BOOKS2READ

Connecting independent readers to independent writers.

Did you love *From Stethoscope to Wisdom*? Then you should read *Footprints in Time*[1] by Dr Andrew C S Koh!

Footprints in Time is a beautifully crafted journey through the landscapes of memory, nostalgia, and the fleeting nature of time. In this deeply reflective narrative, the author invites readers to explore the moments that shape our lives, the people who leave lasting impressions, and the places that hold pieces of our hearts. Each chapter serves as a window into the past, offering glimpses of cherished memories, forgotten dreams, and the quiet beauty of moments once lived but never truly gone.

With lyrical prose and poignant insights, *Footprints in Time* weaves together personal stories with universal themes, creating a tapestry of human experience that resonates with anyone who has ever looked

---

1. https://books2read.com/u/mvVaBj

2. https://books2read.com/u/mvVaBj

back with a mix of longing, gratitude, and introspection. Through the lens of nostalgia, the book explores how time, both fleeting and eternal, imprints itself on our souls, leaving behind footprints that guide us forward even as we remember where we've been.

At its core, *Footprints in Time* is a meditation on the passage of life, the connections we form, and the indelible marks left by the moments that matter most. Whether revisiting childhood memories, reflecting on lost loves, or contemplating the wisdom gained through years of living, this book offers readers the chance to reconnect with their own pasts and rediscover the powerful emotions that time has not erased. It's a celebration of the stories that live on within us, long after the moments have passed.

Read more at https://www.drandrewcskoh.com.

Also by Dr Andrew C S Koh

Bible Study

From Creation to Covenant

From Deceiver to Destiny: Jacob's Story

From Slavery to Freedom

From Man to Mission

From Slave to Brother

From Symbols to Salvation

From Legalism to Liberty

Daily Devotion

Manna of Life: Daily Devotion

Daily Devotions

Bread of Life Daily Devotions

Words of Eternal Life

Bread From Heaven: Daily Devotions

Light of the World Daily Devotions

Light of the World Daily Devotions

The Way, the Truth, and the Life

Genesis
Understanding Genesis 1-11: From Adam to Abraham
Faith Journey of Abraham: Genesis 12-25
Life Story of Jacob: Genesis 26-36
The Story of Joseph: Genesis 37-50
From Pit to Palace

Gospels and Act
The Gospel According to Matthew
Daily Devotion Gospel of Mark
The Gospel According to Luke
Daily Devotion Gospel of John
Acts: Volume 1 and 2, From Jerusalem to Rome
From Galilee to Golgotha

Non Pauline and General Epistles
Hebrews: the Just Shall Live by Faith
1 John, 2 John, 3 John & Jude: a Verse by Verse Bible Study
General Epistles: 1 Peter, 2 Peter, James

Pauline Epistles
Romans: The Just Shall Live by Faith
1 Corinthians
2 Corinthians
1 Thessalonians, 2 Thessalonians, Philemon
Pastoral Epistles: 1 Timothy, 2 Timothy, Titus

Galatians: Justified by Faith in Jesus Christ
Philemon: Charge to the Master's Account

Prison Epistles
The Prison Epistles
Philippians: Rejoice Always in the Lord
Colossians: He is the Image of the Invisible God
Ephesians: Every Spiritual Blessing in the Heavenly Places in Christ

Standalone
Apocalypse: Understanding the Book of Revelation
Expository Preaching
Memoirs of a Doctor
Moses: Let My People Go
Living Word Living Savior: a Portrait of Jesus Through the Eyes of
John
From Stethoscope to Wisdom
Walking in His Footsteps: A Pilgrim's Journey
Journey in Ryhme: Poems of Reflection
Mapping the Heart: The Doctor's Odyssey
The Forgotten Melody
Footprints in Time
From Love to Light

Watch for more at https://www.drandrewcskoh.com.

About the Author

Dr Andrew C S Koh a retired cardiologist, Bible teacher, and author of over 45 Christian books. With a passion for making Scripture come alive, he blends theological insight with practical life application to help readers grow in faith and understanding. His writing reflects a deep commitment to God's Word, forged through decades of medical service, spiritual study, and personal devotion. Dr. Koh's works have encouraged believers around the world to walk closer with Christ and live out their calling with purpose and conviction.

Koh's unique perspective blends his extensive knowledge of the medical field with his deep theological insights. He studied theology at Laidlaw College in Auckland, New Zealand. He now calls Malaysia home, where he lives with his family. He made history in 2021 by setting a record in the Malaysia Book of Records for publishing the most books in a single year.

Whether he's teaching the Bible, creating digital content, or sharing his thoughts through various media, Dr. Koh's mission is clear: to make the Word of God accessible and relevant to everyday life. His works aim to inspire believers to grow deeper in their faith, live with purpose, and embrace the transformative power of God's love.

Link tree:

https://linktr.ee/andrewcskoh

https://books.drandrewcskoh.com/link-tree

free ebook:

https://storyoriginapp.com/giveaways/b295be58-7736-11ec-ac4b-e34d930c508e

Read more at https://www.drandrewcskoh.com.

About the Publisher

Dr. Andrew C. S. Koh is an independent publisher with an impressive portfolio of over 40 titles to his name. His works span a wide array of genres, showcasing his versatility and passion for diverse forms of writing. These genres include fiction, where he weaves captivating narratives, and non-fiction, where he explores a variety of thought-provoking subjects. Additionally, Dr. Koh has contributed to the literary world with insightful biographies and memoirs that offer deep reflections on personal journeys and historical figures.

His poetry resonates with readers through its emotional depth and eloquence, while his travel writings transport audiences to far-off destinations, sharing unique perspectives and experiences. Moreover, Dr. Koh has an extensive collection of works in the realms of Bible study and devotionals, offering spiritual guidance and inspiration to those seeking to deepen their faith. With each book, Dr. Koh has made a significant impact on the literary community, enriching readers' lives with his diverse and thoughtful publications.

Read more at https://www.drandrewcskoh.com.

* 9 7 9 8 2 2 7 2 3 5 3 6 7 *